Ramayana Secrets

Timeless Truths for All

*Profound reflections and hidden wisdom embedded
within the grand epic for inner transformation*

Ramesh Krishna Kumar

ISBN
Paperback 979-8-89556-493-6
Hardcase 979-8-89556-494-3

Contents

Preface and Acknowledgements

"Ramayana Secrets" transcends mere historical recounting to delve into the allegorical spiritual struggles that each of us encounters. While the Ramayana has long been revered for its epic narrative and moral lessons, I felt a compelling need to explore a hidden layer of "facts" that the story might be illustrating, facts that are not just about external events but about the inner dynamics of the human psyche. The characters in the Ramayana, I believe, primarily represent traits within a person, making their battles and triumphs deeply relevant to our own spiritual journeys. Hence, this exploration seeks to bring that aspect to light.

In this book, I portray Rama not just as a historical hero but as a symbol of our higher inner self, grappling with Ravana, who epitomizes our lower instincts—those impulses that drag us into ignorance and fear. Figures like Sugriva and Hanuman exemplify the emotional and devotional sides of our psyche, steering us towards self-discipline and enlightenment, culminating in a personal 'Rama Rajya' under Vibhishana's moderate rule of our senses-driven inner kingdom, Lanka.

The tradition of Ramlila, along with myriad local folklore and arts, vividly showcases the Ramayana's profound influence across Indian and Southeast Asian cultures. This narrative, drawn from Valmiki's epic, honours both the spiritual, devotional, and historical dimensions of these iconic figures, recognizing their significance both metaphysically and geographically.

Drawing on Vedic teachings about the interactions between the atman (soul), mind, and body, this book employs the metaphor of the "churning of the internal milky ocean" to explore these relationships. Just as the gods and demons churned the ocean to unearth treasures, we too must delve into our inner selves—our thoughts, emotions, and spirit—to uncover hidden wisdom and virtues. This book simplifies complex spiritual concepts from the Ramayana, making them accessible to a global audience.

Inspired by my deep connection with characters like Hanuman and Sita, and the impact of sharing their stories with my three-year-old grandson, Dhruv, this journey into the Ramayana's spiritual essence seeks to resonate with readers worldwide.

This work is the result of deep reflection and the invaluable support of many. I am especially grateful to my son and wife, Anand and Lakshmi, whose insights helped shape my thoughts; my sister-in-law, Anuradha, and Shalini Pillay, for their critical editorial guidance; and my friends, too numerous to name, whose influence has been profound. Special thanks to my late parents, sister, and close relatives for their unwavering support. A heartfelt mention goes to my grandson Dhruv, along with son in law and daughter, Praveen and Amritha, whose desire to hear the stories of Hanuman inspired me to embark on this journey.

In our times, filled with moral and societal challenges, the lessons of the Ramayana are incredibly relevant. It is my hope that "Ramayana Secrets" will offer fresh perspectives on these ancient teachings, providing guidance for today's seekers.

May this book encourage you to rediscover the Ramayana, appreciate its spiritual depth, and recognize its enduring relevance.

Happy reading!

Summary

"Ramayana Secrets" interprets the ancient epic by delving into an abstract layer that portrays the characters of Rama, Ravana, and the Vanaras as aspects within an individual's psyche. The book presents the Ramayana as the inner battle between one's higher self (Rama) and the ego-driven, sensory pursuits (Ravana).

The dominant ego, symbolized by Ravana, is the reason for Rama's exile, reflecting how we are disconnected from our divine nature until the events of the Ramayana play out within us. Ravana's abduction of Sita represents the ego's attempt to control spiritual power, and Rama's quest to reclaim her symbolizes the journey to overcome the ego and reunite with the divine self. It is a metaphor for the internal struggle to conquer material desires and return to a life guided by spiritual truth.

The Vanaras represent the emotional and devotional mind that, when aligned, support the journey towards self-realization. Sita symbolizes the inherent power within that guides transformation. The war is not an external event but a metaphor for the inner struggle individuals faces throughout life to reveal their true, divine nature—the Rama within.

Through this lens, the book also addresses common criticisms of Rama, offering a deeper understanding of his actions. It emphasizes the contemporary relevance of the Ramayana, offering lessons that can be applied from youth to adulthood.

In an appendix, this interpretation of the Ramayana is presented as a potential framework for a psychology theory, one that goes deeper into the human psyche than Western approaches. The book remains faithful to the original Valmiki Ramayana, by excluding other retellings, to preserve the purity of the text's profound wisdom. Understanding the Ramayana in this depth, the book argues, is crucial for navigating modern life with insight and spiritual growth.

It is important to understand Sita, "shakti", commonly used to describe the inner power or divine energy that drives transformation or the pursuit of a cause. In Sanskrit, Shakti refers to the inherent power or force within an individual that enables change, growth, and action. It is often associated with the divine feminine energy that brings about transformation and is a key concept in many spiritual traditions, particularly in Hindu philosophy.

In Valmiki's Ramayana, the emotional mind is symbolized by the monkey-like Vanaras, whose exhilaration in the forest reflects the restless search for meaning, while the ego is portrayed through the Rakshasas, embodying profane tendencies and desires; Valmiki's creative portrayals of these inner struggles remain profound and unexplainable.

"Ramayana Secrets" is for readers seeking a deeper, more introspective understanding of the Ramayana beyond its surface-level narrative. It is ideal for those who are curious about the inner spiritual journey and wish to explore the symbolic meaning behind Rama, Ravana, and the Vanaras as aspects of the self. This book speaks to those interested in personal transformation, spiritual growth, and psychological insights rooted in ancient wisdom, offering practical lessons that apply from youth to adulthood. By focusing solely on the original Valmiki Ramayana, "Ramayana Secrets" stays true to the epic's foundational messages while revealing their relevance in modern life.

Prologue

At the core of the Ramayana is dharma—a complex concept of moral duty that guides every action. To help explain this, I turn to the later epic, the Mahabharata, and the story of Karna. Though his tale unfolds many Yugas after the Ramayana, Karna's struggles with duty, honour, and loyalty provide insight into the challenges of understanding dharma. Through these epics, we can begin to explore the layered meaning of dharma that shapes the Ramayana's narrative.

In the land of Bharata, the principles of dharma weave through the lives of its people like an invisible thread, guiding their actions and decisions. The epic tales of the Ramayana and the Mahabharata are replete with moments where this elusive concept is tested and illuminated. One such poignant intersection is found in the life and death of Karna, a noble warrior from the Mahabharata, whose struggles and questions echo the trials faced by Lord Rama described in the Ramayana of an earlier era.

As dawn broke over the battlefield of Kurukshetra, Karna lay wounded, his life's blood ebbing away. His chariot was broken, and an arrow pierced his jugular. His thoughts, however, were not on his impending death but on the weight of his decisions and the complexity of his dharma. He gazed up at the sky, seeking answers that had eluded him throughout his life.

Lord Krishna, the charioteer of Arjuna, Karna's Nemesis, approached him, his serene presence a stark contrast to the chaos around. With a voice both gentle and profound, Krishna began to unravel the intricate tapestry of dharma. Karna's life, marked by many noble qualities yet shadowed by his loyalty to Duryodhana, the usurper, selfish antagonist and antihero of the Mahabharata.

"Why, Krishna?" Karna's voice trembled with the weight of his query. "Why must I, who have adhered to dharma in many ways, meet such a tragic end?"

Krishna's eyes softened with compassion. "Karna, dharma is not just about individual actions but about the greater cosmic order. Your life was a testament to nobility, talent and generosity, yet it was also intertwined with adharma through your allegiance to Duryodhana. True dharma transcends the immediate, seeking to uphold the balance and well-being of the universe."

Karna's confusion deepened. "But what about my Svadharma, my personal duty as a warrior and friend? Did I not fulfil that?"

"Svadharma, your personal duty, is indeed crucial," Krishna replied. "Yet, it must align with Sanatana dharma, the eternal and universal principles that govern righteousness. Your loyalty to Duryodhana, though rooted in personal duty, conflicted with the higher principles of dharma. This misalignment led to your downfall."

As Karna absorbed Krishna's words, he felt a presence beside him. It was Lord Surya, his divine father, whose radiance seemed to light up the battlefield. Surya's voice was filled with paternal warmth and wisdom. "My son, your life was a constant struggle to reconcile these truths. Vishesa dharma, the specific duties arising from circumstances, also plays a role. Your decisions, influenced by your immediate situation, often overshadowed the broader, universal principles of dharma."

Karna reflected on the adharmic actions he had committed, pointed out by Krishna: his participation in the disrobing of Draupadi, his deceitful killing of Abhimanyu, and his unwavering support for Duryodhana's unjust causes. These actions, though seen as loyalty to his friend, were deviations from the path of righteousness.

These reflections drew a parallel to the trials faced by Lord Rama in the Ramayana. Rama, the epitome of dharma, faced profound tests that questioned the very essence of righteousness. His decision to honour his father's word and accept exile, his heartbreaking choice to send Sita away despite knowing her purity, and his actions during the battle against Ravana— all these moments were shrouded in the complexities of Svadharma, Sanatana dharma, and Vishesa dharma.

In a land far from the futurist land Kurukshetra, the kingdom of Ayodhya of an earlier era echoed with the tales of Rama's adherence to dharma. As Rama walked the path of righteousness, his journey mirrored the internal battle faced by every individual—the struggle to uphold personal duty, universal principles, and situational ethics amidst personal trials and societal expectations.

"Ramayana Secrets" delves into these layers of meaning, revealing the profound wisdom embedded in the epic. It explores how Rama's actions, often questioned and critiqued, align with the higher principles of dharma. The narrative invites us to see beyond the surface, to recognize the deeper truths about duty, righteousness, and the eternal quest for spiritual enlightenment.

As you embark on this journey through the pages of "Ramayana Secrets," you will uncover the timeless relevance of the Ramayana. It is not merely a historical recount but a mirror reflecting the complexities of our own spiritual journey, urging us to integrate our highest values into every aspect of life. The epic's teachings on dharma and the interconnectedness of all beings remain a beacon of wisdom for the past, present, and future.

Chapter 1

Introduction

This rendition of the Ramayana explores the epic through the Vedic concept of oneness, presenting creation's elements—divine, profane, sensory—as interconnected. The characters, including Rama, Lakshman, Ravana, and others, are depicted not just as story figures but as representations of facets of our own consciousness and existence, that amounts to our oneness and the struggle between our higher aspirations and baser instincts.

The Ramayana narrative, rich with conflicts and resolutions, portrays a journey of self-discovery and spiritual realization, emphasizing how each character's story reflects our inner battles and growth towards oneness achieving our true divine nature. "Ramayana Secrets" reveals the profound layers of wisdom in these ancient tales, encouraging readers to look beyond the narrative and discover the eternal truths embedded within everyone, relevant across all ages.

The Ramayana's style is encapsulated in the verse "पुरावृत्तं कथायुक्तमितिहासं प्रचक्षते" (Purvayuktam Kathayuktam Itihasam

Pracakshateh), meaning "ancient events, narrated as stories to explain the way things happened."

This defines *"itihasa"*—a term that translates to narrating historical events through engaging stories that illustrate the philosophy of life, offering principles (facts) that can be applied to one's own life. This storytelling approach makes profound teachings accessible to everyone. The epic features a diverse cast of characters, from the articulate Vanaras to the complex Rakshasas, weaving together themes of separation, longing, abduction, and resolution.

To fully appreciate "Ramayana Secrets," one must view the Ramayana as more than a historical account confined to the Treta Yuga. Instead, it should be seen as an inner journey, a timeless narrative that transcends its ancient setting and remains relevant across eras, offering wisdom that can guide one's life today.

Rama, Sita, Ravana, and Hanuman symbolize the traits and conflicts within each of us, reflecting the human struggle with righteousness, temptation, and personal growth. In this perspective, Rama embodies dharma and our true self, Sita represents the guiding force of faith, and Ravana personifies our lower impulses driven by ego and desire.

Beneath the surface of these engaging stories lie principles that guide individual human lives, offering valuable lessons that can be applied to our own journey toward spiritual enlightenment.

Ravana represents hedonism and egoism, ruling over the metaphorical kingdom of Lanka within everyone. This realm is dominated by the pursuit of worldly pleasures, driven by lust, greed, pride, and power, reflecting a disregard for higher values and divine nature. Ramayana provides guidance on overcoming these negative traits, promoting a journey towards righteousness and inner divinity.

It portrays Hanuman as the embodiment of unwavering devotion, whose efforts to rescue Sita symbolize the inner spiritual journey to reconnect with our divine essence. His attributes of strength, selflessness, and loyalty are highlighted as essential qualities for overcoming the ego and achieving spiritual enlightenment

For readers interested in a summary of the portrayal of various key Ramayana characters and their corresponding inner traits as interpreted in this book, Part B of the Epilogue provides a quick overview

Hanuman exemplifies the quintessence of "devotion-bhakti" in Valmiki's Ramayana through various key events. His profound intelligence and tact first come to light in *Kishkindha Kanda*, where he meets Rama and Lakshman disguised as a sage, deftly negotiating an alliance that shapes the course of the epic. By *Sundara Kanda*, Hanuman's courage and loyalty are prominently displayed when he makes the audacious leap to Lanka, a daring act of devotion to Rama's cause. His clever manoeuvres in Lanka, from searching for Sita to navigating through enemies, highlight his unwavering commitment and resourceful nature. These acts are not merely displays of physical bravery but are underscored by a deep spiritual devotion, illustrating Hanuman's integral role in the epic's exploration of good versus evil.

Hanuman humbly acknowledged that the extraordinary feats he had accomplished—crossing the ocean, infiltrating Lanka, and finding Sita—were all due to Rama's divine power. He attributed his strength and success entirely to Rama's grace, explaining that his abilities reflected Rama's power working through him. This humility and recognition of divine influence underscore the depth of Hanuman's bhakti, reinforcing his role as a symbol of ultimate devotion.

To fully engage with the themes of this book, one should connect with the **Hanuman within**, discovering personal capacities for devotion and righteousness. The image of Rama and Sita residing in Hanuman's heart symbolizes the deep internalization of divine love and duty, offering a powerful metaphor for personal spiritual growth. Hanuman's example invites readers to explore their potential for spiritual growth and recognize that true strength comes from aligning with higher, divine principles.

Note: **Goddess Sita**

In Indian philosophy, Goddesses symbolizes the divine energy known as Shakti, essential for the universe's operation. Goddess Sita's role in the Ramayana transcends the ideal wife, she represents an active, vital force that drives spiritual growth and inner divinity. This "Shakti" that keeps us rooted, urging a deep, personal transformation aligned with spiritual advancement.

Sita's journey encourages us to harmonize our actions with higher spiritual principles, navigating life's complexities with wisdom and grace. By embracing and integrating these energies within us, we unlock pathways to enlightenment and a richer understanding of our spiritual journey. In fact, Ramayana is also known as "Sitayana" or "Sita Charita" – Sita's Journey or Sita's Story -focuses on Sita's life and experiences, particularly emphasizing her trials, abduction by Ravana, and her unwavering fidelity to Rama

Valmiki's Sloka

Valmiki's famous utterance on seeing the krauncha birds is found in the beginning of the Ramayana, where Valmiki witnesses the killing of a mating pair of krauncha birds. The verse (shloka) from the Ramayana

"मा निषाद प्रतिष्ठां त्वम् अगमः शाश्वतीः समाः।

यत् क्रौंचमिथुनादेकम् अवधीः काममोहितम्॥"

mā niṣāda pratiṣṭhāṁ tvamagamaḥ śāśvatīḥ samāḥ

yat krauñcamithunādekam avadhīḥ kāmamohitam

Oh hunter, may you repent for life and suffer, find no rest or fame, for you have killed one of the unsuspecting, devoted and loving krauñcha couple.

This incident serves as a catalyst for Valmiki's transformation from a hunter to a sage and the narration style called sloka.

A metaphorical and allegorical meaning

The phrase "Maa Nishada," uttered by Valmiki upon witnessing the sorrowful plight of the Krauncha birds, holds a profound metaphorical and allegorical meaning.

Metaphorically, "Maa Nishada" reflects the human experience of separation and loss in the pursuit of sensory pleasures and worldly desires. It symbolizes the lament of the soul caught in the transient and often painful nature of material existence. The hunter, in this metaphor, can be seen as Lord Shiva—the lord of destruction and regeneration. As the destroyer of illusions and the force behind transformation, Shiva's role as the hunter signifies the inevitable disruptions in life that awaken us to deeper spiritual realities.

The sorrowful lament of "Maa Nishada" underlines the pathos and profound sense of loss that accompany our earthly journey. It serves as a reminder that during our engrossment in impermanent sensory pursuits, we often face moments of intense pain and separation, prompting a deeper reflection on the transient nature of worldly attachments.

Thus, this Krauncha Bird episode illustrates the essential human condition—wherein the pursuit of ephemeral pleasures can lead to suffering and separation from your inherent divine nature yet holds the potential for spiritual awakening and transformation. The hunter's arrow, while causing pain, ultimately serves as a catalyst for regeneration and spiritual growth, guiding us towards a higher state of consciousness and inner peace.

Chapter 2

A Summary of the Overall Storyline

The early phase of the Valmiki Ramayana primarily revolves around King Dasharatha, the ruler of Ayodhya, who is depicted as a just and powerful king but troubled by his childlessness. Despite having three wives, Kaushalya, Sumitra, and Kaikeyi, Dasharatha lacks an heir to continue his lineage, which casts a shadow over his otherwise prosperous and stable reign.

The urgency for an heir is amplified by Dasharatha's responsibility to the Ishvaku dynasty. Renowned for its righteous rule, the continuity of this lineage is crucial for maintaining dharma and divine favour in the kingdom. The potential end of this lineage posed a threat not only to familial legacy but also to the cosmic order and societal stability of Ayodhya.

Driven by his desire for progeny, Dasharatha performs the sacred Putrakameshti Yajna, a ritual imploring the gods for the gift of children. The ritual invokes divine intervention, and as a result, the god of fire appears and gives Dasharatha a pot of sacred porridge. His wives consume this porridge, leading to the miraculous birth of four sons—Rama, born to Kaushalya; Bharata, born to Kaikeyi; and the twins Lakshman and Shatrughna, born to Sumitra. These children are considered divine gifts, destined for greatness. The early life of Rama and his brothers in Ayodhya is marked by their education and training in both scholarly and martial disciplines, under the guidance of sage Vasishta. They grow up displaying remarkable virtues and skills, endearing themselves to the populace of Ayodhya.

The narrative takes a significant turn with the arrival of Sage Vishwamitra, who requests Dasharatha's help to protect his sacred rituals from the demons Maricha and Subahu. Initially hesitant, Dasharatha is persuaded by Vishwamitra and his advisor Vasishta to send Rama, who is still a young boy, and Lakshman to aid the sage. This event marks the beginning of Rama's adventures and his emergence as a hero.

The decision to assist Vishwamitra reflects Dasharatha's growing need to establish a worthy successor. His counsel and subjects view Rama's capability to protect the sage's yajna as proof of his potential and worthiness as the future king. The successful protection of the yajna and the subsequent slaying of the demons significantly elevate Rama's stature both as a divine figure and a capable leader in the eyes of Ayodhya's people and the royal court.

These early episodes lay the foundational virtues of heroism, obedience, and dharma that characterize Rama, setting the stage for his later exploits and trials in the epic.

Delving Deeper....

As King Dasharatha nears the twilight of his reign, he contemplates the future stability and prosperity of Ayodhya. Realizing the importance of appointing a successor who could continue his legacy, his thoughts naturally turn to his eldest son, Rama, whom he sees as the ideal candidate. To ensure a wise and balanced decision, Dasharatha calls a meeting with his council of ministers to discuss the matter and seek their opinions.

Dasharatha: "Esteemed members of the council, the time has come for us to consider the future of our beloved Ayodhya. I have been pondering the matter of my succession, and my heart tells me that Rama, my eldest, is ready to take on the mantle of kingship. He has shown himself to be wise, just, and capable. But as always, I seek your counsel. What are your thoughts on his suitability to be our next king?"

Council Member 1: "O Great King, your thoughts resonate well with the sentiments of your council. Rama's virtues are widely recognized not only within these walls but also across our kingdom. His profound understanding of dharma and his adherence to truth set him apart as a leader moulded for kingship."

Council Member 2: "Indeed, my lord, Rama embodies the ideal qualities of a king. His recent protection of Sage Vishwamitra's yajna from the demons has not only proven his valour but also his commitment to protecting our spiritual heritage and the welfare of the realm."

Council Member 3: "His wisdom in dealing with the subjects, his unfailing respect towards his elders, and his kindness towards the young and old alike ensure that he is a prince who has already won the hearts of the people. A king who holds the love of his subjects holds the key to a prosperous and peaceful reign."

Council Member 4: "Moreover, King, Rama's ability to inspire and lead with compassion while adhering firmly to the principles of justice assures us that he will be a ruler who can navigate the challenges of kingship with the same balance and fairness as you have, revered Dasharatha."

Dasharatha: "Your insights are invaluable and reinforce my belief that Rama is indeed the right choice to lead Ayodhya after me. It is reassuring to hear your strong support for his ascension. We must now proceed to prepare him and our kingdom for this auspicious transition. I am grateful for your wise counsel and steadfast loyalty."

The council's resounding approval and enthusiastic endorsements solidify Dasharatha's decision, initiating the meticulous preparations for Rama's coronation. This collective endorsement reflects a deep commitment to the continued stability and flourishing of Ayodhya, with the anticipation of a prosperous era under Rama's leadership.

With this solid foundation, we swiftly move forward to delve deeper into the epic of the Ramayana. This journey through the lives of Rama, Sita, and their companions allows us to explore the profound layers and hidden meanings embedded in the saga of this divine avatar.

As the narrative unfolds, it invites us to uncover the spiritual and moral lessons that remain relevant across ages and cultures, highlighting the timeless relevance of the Ramayana in understanding duty, righteousness, and the complexities of human and divine actions.

An overview

The story of Rama, Sita, and their adventures unfolds in several key sections, called Kand (Book, Chapter) of the Ramayana.

Prince Rama, the eldest son of King Dasharatha of Ayodhya, is on the verge of being crowned king when his stepmother, Kaikeyi, invokes a past promise made by Dasharatha, leading to Rama's exile. In a testament to their devotion and loyalty, his wife Sita and brother Lakshman choose to join him, accompanying Rama to the forest for a 14-year exile.

In the forest, the trio leads a simple life, encountering sages, demons, and various challenges. Their peace is shattered when the demon king Ravana abducts Sita and takes her to his kingdom, Lanka.

Rama and Lakshman form an alliance with Hanuman and the Vanara king Sugriva, who agree to help find Sita. Hanuman's devotion to Rama shines through as he leaps across the ocean to Lanka, finds Sita, and assures her of Rama's impending rescue.

Hanuman's journey to Lanka is filled with feats of strength and devotion. He sets Lanka ablaze after delivering Rama's message to Sita, showcasing his heroic efforts.

Rama, with an army of Vanaras and bears, builds a bridge to Lanka. A fierce battle ensues, and Rama ultimately defeats Ravana, liberating Sita.

Rama, Sita, and Lakshman return to Ayodhya, where Rama is crowned king, initiating a period of peace and prosperity known as Rama-Rajya, despite Sita passing a trial by fire to prove her purity. Due to societal pressures Rama had to exile a pregnant Sita. She finds refuge in sage Valmiki's ashram, where she gives birth to twins, Lava and Kusha. Years later, the twins are reunited with Rama. Seeking solace, Sita returns to the earth, her mother.

The Ramayana concludes with Rama's continued rule over Ayodhya, epitomizing the ideals of justice, righteousness, and compassion.

Throughout the epic, Hanuman, the devoted servant of Rama, plays a pivotal role. His loyalty, strength, and devotion make him a crucial figure in the rescue of Sita and the defeat of Ravana, embodying the virtues of selfless service and unwavering faith.

Delving Deeper....

"Ramayana Secrets: Timeless Truths for All" presents the Valmiki Ramayana as a powerful allegory of human spiritual growth. Lord Rama, representing the true self, embarks on a journey to conquer Ravana, the embodiment of ego and base tendencies. This epic is more than just a story of battles— it portrays inner transformation and the restoration of harmony within.

Aided by the Vanaras, symbolizing the untamed mind, Rama's trials reflect our own spiritual challenges. The narrative urges us to rise above selfish desires by adhering to dharma, fostering virtues like righteousness, courage, and wisdom. Ravana, driven by ego and materialism, embodies the struggle between temptation and ethical living, offering a timeless lesson in overcoming negativity to attain spiritual enlightenment.

The inner Divine (Rama) and inherent faith (Sita)

Rama symbolizes the divine nature and inherent goodness within us all, while Sita represents the deep faith and moral integrity every person holds. Together, they exemplify the highest ideals of righteousness and truth that define human nature. Sita's unwavering trust and faith guide us towards a virtuous path. Life's journey, filled with challenges and encounters with our darker selves, mirrors the mythological churning of the milky ocean, reflecting our internal struggles and growth.

Let us list out the divine qualities every human being possesses, they are the sixteen divine qualities of Rama explained by Sage Narada in BalaKanda chapter one

1. Gunavaan (Virtuous)

2. Viryavaan (Courageous)

3. Dharmajnah (Righteous)

4. Kritajnah(Grateful)

5. Satyavaakyah (Truthful)

6. Dhrdhavratah (Steadfast)

7. Caritravaan (Good Character)

8. Sarvabhuteshu Hitah (Auspicious to All)

9. Vidvan (Knowledgeable)

10. Samarthah (Capable)

11. Priyadarshanah (Attractive)

12. Atmavaan (Self-controlled)

13. Jitakrodhah (Conqueror of Anger)

14. Dyutiman (Resplendent)

15. Anasuyakah (Free of Envy)

16. Bibhyatidevah (Revered by Gods)

Here are specific examples from Valmiki's Ramayana that illustrate Lord Rama's 16 traits that explain why Rama is a revered ideal personality.

1. **Gunavaan (Virtuous)** - Rama's virtues are described in ***Bala Kanda*** when Sage Vishwamitra praises him before King Dasharatha while asking to take him to protect the yajna from demons (Chapter 20).

2. **Viryavaan (Courageous)** - Rama demonstrates his courage in ***Aranya Kanda*** when he fights and defeats the demoness Shurpanakha and her brothers Khara and Dushana (Chapter 22-24).

3. **Dharmajnah (Righteous)** - In ***Ayodhya Kanda***, Rama decides to go to exile for 14 years to honour his father's promise to Kaikeyi, embodying his commitment to dharma (Chapter 19-20)

4. **Kritajnah (Grateful)** - In ***Kishkindha Kanda***, Rama shows gratitude to Hanuman for finding Sita and bringing her jewel as proof (Chapter 41).

5. **Satyavaakyah (Truthful)** - Throughout the epic, Rama's commitment to speaking the truth is evident, particularly in ***Yuddha Kanda*** when he reassures Vibhishana of his support against Ravana (Chapter 17).

6. **Dhrdhavratah (Steadfast)** - Rama's steadfast nature is seen in ***Yuddha Kanda*** as he prepares to battle Ravana despite the odds (Chapter 89).

7. **Caritravaan (Good Character)** - In *Ayodhya Kanda*, Rama's respectful interaction with his parents and his adherence to their wishes demonstrate his good character (Chapter 20).

8. **Sarvabhuteshu Hitah (Auspicious to All)** - Rama's actions for the benefit of all creatures are highlighted in *Sundara Kanda*, where he vows to protect all sages and innocents from demon harassment (Chapter 35).

9. **Vidvan (Knowledgeable)** - Rama displays his knowledge and wisdom during his conversation with Sage Agastya in *Aranya Kanda*, where he discusses various philosophical concepts (Chapter 11).

10. **Samarthah (Capable)** - His capability as a leader and warrior is demonstrated in *Yuddha Kanda* during the planning and execution of the bridge to Lanka (Chapter 22).

11. **Priyadarshanah (Attractive)** - Rama's attractive appearance is often mentioned; in *Sundara Kanda*, even Ravana admires Rama's form when he sees his reflection (Chapter 36).

12. **Atmavaan (Self-controlled)** - Rama's self-control is evident in *Ayodhya Kanda*, where he calmly accepts the news of his exile without anger (Chapter 19).

13. **Jitakrodhah (Conqueror of Anger)** - Despite provocations from demons and adversities, Rama often keeps his composure, especially noticeable in *Aranya Kanda* when facing Shurpanakha (Chapter 17).

14. **Dyutiman (Resplendent)** - Rama's radiance is described during his wedding in *Bala Kanda*, where he is said to shine forth among the princes (Chapter 73).

15. **Anasuyakah (Free of Envy)** - Rama shows no envy towards Bharata when Bharata comes to persuade him to return to Ayodhya and rule the kingdom in *Ayodhya Kanda* (Chapter 100).

16. **Bibhyatidevah (Revered by Gods)** - Throughout the epic, gods including Brahma and Shiva praise Rama, and in *Yuddha Kanda*, they watch his battle with Ravana with admiration (Chapter 108).

Ravana

In the Valmiki Ramayana, Ravana is portrayed as a being who has existed for many yugas, making him extraordinarily ancient, while Rama, in stark contrast, is very young—only 16 years old when he embarks on his journey with Vishwamitra. This age difference symbolizes more than just a generational gap; it suggests that Ravana represents deep-rooted, preexisting traits within the human psyche, traits that have persisted across ages.

Meanwhile, Rama embodies the youthful, emerging force of righteousness and divine consciousness. Their battle is not merely a clash between contemporaries but a timeless struggle between entrenched negative tendencies and the fresh, virtuous spirit of new potential that human consciousness develops. This layered interpretation supports the abstract, symbolic treatment of their conflict presented in this book.

Ravana, the rakshasa king, personifies sensory hedonistic traits and worldly desires that seek to possess faith (Sita) and draw it away from its divine source (Rama). His abduction of Sita illustrates how sensory pleasures and material temptations can lead one astray from their true divine nature, causing inner turmoil and suffering. Ravana's qualities, such as arrogance, lust, deceitfulness, tyranny, disrespect for women, lack of empathy, and hubris, are emblematic of the darker aspects of human nature that disrupt moral behaviour and cause harm.

Lanka, as ruled by Ravana, serves as an allegorical kingdom dominated by sensory, egoistic tendencies. These traits are not just individual flaws but represent broader forces that have existed within the human experience for eons, making the battle between Rama and Ravana a symbolic struggle between the eternal forces of divine and profane within. This abstract treatment of Ravana as a representation of these qualities makes sense, given his ancient existence and the symbolic nature of his character.

Some of the qualities of Ravana that can be summarised

1. Arrogance (pride)

2. Lust (desire, and a lack of respect for the sanctity of marriage)

3. Deceitfulness (trickery and deception)

4. Tyranny (ruthless pursuit of power) going to any lengths to maintain control.

5. Disrespect for women (viewing them as a possession)

6. Lack of empathy (own selfish desires supreme)

7. Hubris (blind to his own weaknesses)

The Ramayana as presented to symbolize the dynamics of the human psyche, reflecting the intricate traits within everyone's inner world. This epic showcases the noble qualities of Rama and Sita as facets of our higher self, contrasted with our baser instincts represented by the egoistic sensory persona. It captures the ever-changing nature of our emotions, devotion, and instincts, all housed within our thoughts. Thus, the Ramayana unfolds internally, from the enlightenment of human consciousness by Rama's avatar. Readers are encouraged to see the epic's characters not just as historical figures, but as reflections of their own inner selves, embodying emotions and thought processes. This insight invites profound personal reflection, seeing the Ramayana as a mirror to our psyche, the core of our individual identity.

Note of Ravana's inherent nature

In the Uttara Kanda of the Valmiki Ramayana, Ravana's inherent nature as a figure of boundless greed and unchecked ambition is vividly depicted through his ruthless seizure of the kingdom and immense wealth of his stepbrother, Kubera, the god of wealth. This act of sheer aggression and moral corruption is not merely an instance of lust for power but a profound reflection of Ravana's deep-seated disregard for righteousness and justice.

Ravana, driven by an insatiable desire for dominance, did not hesitate to betray familial bonds and the principles of dharma that he should have upheld. His conquest of Lanka, once the prosperous domain of Kubera, was marked by a brutal and unprincipled usurpation that left Kubera with no choice but to flee to the city of Alaka. This was not just the takeover of a kingdom; it was an assault on the very fabric of familial loyalty and the cosmic order that sustains righteousness.

Ravana's moral corruption extended beyond political tyranny; his personal life was equally tainted by acts of violence and immorality. He molested many women, forcefully keeping them in his harem, and his rape of Rambha, a celestial nymph, earned him a curse that later prevented him from similarly violating Sita. This curse reflected his own self-interest, driven by the fear of further divine retribution rather than any genuine moral restraint.

Ravana's rule, characterized by injustice and the trampling of dharma, is portrayed as inherently unstable and destined to collapse under the weight of its own corruption. His story underscores a central theme of the Ramayana: that moral corruption and the abandonment of righteousness lead inevitably to ruin, no matter how powerful one may seem. Ravana's fate was sealed not by the might of his enemies, but by the inherent flaws in his own character, making his story a timeless allegory of the dangers of unchecked ambition and moral decay.

The portrayal of Ravana as "just" in certain interpretations of the Ramayana offers a nuanced view. However, it's important to note that such depictions are not in line with the original Valmiki Ramayana, where Ravana is primarily portrayed as a symbol of ego and moral corruption.

Ravana is depicted as a figure whose actions were largely driven by his desires, ego, and misuse of power, which are fundamentally at odds with the concept of justice.

Ravana's abduction of Sita, a central act in the epic, was done against her will and was an act of deceit and power, clearly violating principles of justice and righteousness. Additionally, his rule in Lanka, while prosperous, was marked by tyranny and oppression, indicating a reign that prioritized power and fear over equitable governance. Ravana's refusal to return Sita peacefully, despite numerous advisories and opportunities to correct his wrongdoing, further showcases his disregard for moral and ethical standards.

Moreover, Ravana's actions led to suffering not only among his enemies but also among his own people, who eventually faced the devastation of war because of his decisions. His rule, although sometimes described as strong and effective, was fundamentally self-serving and did not truly embody the virtues of a just ruler, such as fairness, moral integrity, and concern for the welfare of all subjects.

This contrasts sharply with the virtuous leadership of Rama.

Another depiction portrays Ravana as a "just" Dravidian ruler, which can sometimes be a misleading attempt by certain groups to fuel the Aryan-Dravidian divide. Such interpretations, explore traits that deviate from Valmiki's original portrayal.

In "Ramayana Secrets," by examining the Ramayana at a deeper, more abstract level, these divisive portrayals are rendered irrelevant, focusing instead on the universal themes and true insights of the epic.

Ravana's great power and invincibility are often attributed to the various boons he received from the gods, including Shiva, which play a significant role in making him the formidable adversary he is portrayed as. However, his ultimate downfall is a reminder that even the greatest boons can be rendered powerless in the face of righteousness and divine will.

Unlike true devotees, whose worship stems from selflessness and reverence, Ravana's piety was a calculated tool for worldly gains, which highlights the irony of his devotion. His story serves as a cautionary tale about the perils of insincere spiritual practices, underlining how such actions not only lead to moral compromise but also set the stage for inevitable downfall. This portrayal challenges the notion of his justice, suggesting that his supposed righteousness was often overshadowed by deeper flaws.

The Story of Ravana's Shiva Tandava Stotra

Though the Valmiki Ramayana does not mention Ravana composing the Shiva Tandava Stotra, it has become an established part of the Ramayana tradition, much like the Lakshman Rekha. Some interesting observations on that narrative.

In the shadowy reaches of the Himalayas, beneath the towering presence of Mount Kailash, a tale of devotion and arrogance unfolds, etching itself into the annals of myth. Ravana, the mighty king of Lanka, fuelled by his boundless ambition and pride, sought to challenge the very limits of his power. His journey led him to the abode of Lord Shiva, where he dared to attempt the unthinkable—to lift Mount Kailash, the celestial mountain itself.

As Ravana placed his hands upon the mountain, his intentions were grandiose. He planned to carry Kailash back to Lanka as a testament to his unmatched strength and to earn Shiva's favour. The mountain began to tremble, sending a deep rumble through the realms of gods and demons alike. However, Lord Shiva, undisturbed and unimpressed by this display of arrogance, pressed down the mountain with the mere touch of his toe.

Trapped under the immense weight of Kailash, Ravana was pinned with crushing force. The pain was immense, and his mighty roars turned to helpless cries. In his anguish and desperation, Ravana's pride crumbled, giving way to a surge of devotion. He realized the folly of his arrogance and sought to appease the great ascetic, Lord Shiva.

In his confinement beneath the mountain, Ravana composed the Shiva Tandava Stotram, a hymn of praise that echoed through the valleys and celestial spheres. His voice, filled with devotion, sang praises of Shiva's infinite qualities, resonating with deep reverence and repentance. The verses he crafted were both a plea for forgiveness and a profound acknowledgment of Shiva's supremacy.

Touched by Ravana's transformation from arrogance to adoration, and moved by the poetic beauty of the hymn, Shiva released Ravana from his confinement. He bestowed upon him the divine sword Chandrahas—a gift of grace yet accompanied by a solemn warning of its potential curse should it be misused.

Thus, from the throes of pride and punishment, arose the Shiva Tandava Stotram, a timeless ode to the complexities of devotion and the eternal dance of destruction and grace, forever reminding Ravana and the world of the fine line between ambition and hubris.

Hanuman: The Power of Devotion

Hanuman, the devoted messenger in service of Rama, represents the power of bhakti (devotion) that is aligned with the inner divinity. His unwavering loyalty, strength, and selfless service are the qualities that help restore faith (Sita) to the divine (Rama). Hanuman's heroic journey and exploits to find Sita signifies the role of devotion in reuniting one's faith with their inner divine nature.

The Battle and Restoration

The fierce battle between Rama and Ravana symbolizes the internal struggle between one's higher self and lower desires. Rama's victory over Ravana signifies the triumph of divine virtues over profane temptations (rakshasa nature). Hanuman's pivotal role in this battle highlights how devotion and spiritual discipline facilitate this inner victory.

Separation, Search an underlying theme

Throughout life, we encounter various episodes of separation that prompt us to search, evolve, and grow. The Ramayana vividly portrays these transformative events.

Rama's Separation When He Was About to Become Prince: This represents the transition from the divine innocence of childhood through the teenage years, a period marked by an exile-like journey into the forest of life, where one searches for identity and purpose.

Rama and Sita's Separation When Abducted by Ravana: During the teenage years, one often loses faith as profane tendencies abduct one's sense of divine self. This symbolizes the internal struggle and the challenges of maintaining one's values amidst external temptations.

Rama Exiling a Pregnant Sita Due to Societal Pressures: Even after subduing profane tendencies, the evolved being continues to face challenges in maintaining a life dedicated to divine pursuits amidst worldly expectations and judgments and hence cannot sustain faith.

Sita's exile and her refuge in sage Valmiki's ashram represent the ongoing trials of faith due to societal pressure. The role of their progeny, Lava and Kusha, exemplifies the need for continuous spiritual resilience amidst life's challenges.

Five Self-Reflection questions

2.1 Can you recognize the 16 divine qualities within you...
self-reflect and score yourself on a scale of 1 to 10 each
of these qualities, these represent your manifested divine
qualities

1. Gunavaan (Virtuous)

2. Viryavaan (Courageous)

3. Dharmajnah (Righteous)

4. Kritajnah(Grateful)

5. Satyavaakyah (Truthful)

6. Dhrdhavratah (Steadfast)

7. Caritravaan (Good Character)

8. Sarvabhuteshu Hitah (Auspicious to All)

9. Vidvan (Knowledgeable)

10. Samarthah (Capable)

11. Priyadarshanah (Attractive)

12. Atmavaan (Self-controlled)

13. Jitakrodhah (Conqueror of Anger)

14. Dyutiman (Resplendent)

15. Anasuyakah (Free of Envy)

16. Bibhyatidevah (Revered by Gods)

2.2 Can you recognize the existence of "Sita" like power within you...self-reflect and score yourself on a scale of 1 to 10 each of these qualities, that define your ability to sustain faith

1. Loyalty:

2. Grace

3. Purity

4. Kindness

5. Courageous

6. Strength

7. Resilience

8. Humility

9. Modesty

10. Wisdom

11. Spirituality

12. Duty bound

2.3 Can you recognize the existence of "Hanuman" like power within you...self-reflect and score yourself on a scale of 1 to 10, each of these qualities define the active devotional power within

1. Steadfast Loyalty

2. Selfless Service

3. Unconditional Love

4. Courage and Bravery

5. Strength and Resilience

6. Humility

7. Unshakable Trust

8. Wisdom

9. Perseverance

10. Determination

11. Kindness

12. Spiritual Insight

13. Adaptability

14. Resourcefulness

15. Patience

16. Inspirational

2.4 Can you recognize the existence of "Ravana" like profane tendencies within you...self-reflect and score yourself on a scale of 1 to 10, each of these qualities are the obstacles you must overcome to become a realized person

1. Greed

2. Pride and Arrogance

3. Lust and Sensuality

4. Deceiving

5. Manipulative

6. Angry and Vengeful

7. Disrespect for the Divine

8. Immoral

9. Self-Centeredness

10. Narcissism

11. Dominance and Control

12. Impatient and Impulsive

13. Unjust

14. Stubborn

15. Refusal to listen to good counsel

16. Dominating

2.5 Can you describe events that were life changing and impacted your life in the past such as: Traumatic Experiences; Stress and Overwork; Negative Relationships: Materialism and Hedonism; Moral and Ethical Dilemmas; Illness and Suffering; Societal Pressures; Loss of Purpose

Reflect, how the below positive actions can counter trauma of these events

- **Cultivating hope, compassion, and a sense of purpose**: By focusing on positive emotions and a higher purpose, individuals *can **overcome feelings of despair, anger, and hopelessness***, thereby restoring inner peace and divine purpose.

- **Engaging in spiritual practices**: Regular meditation, prayer, and acts of kindness nurture one's divine nature, enhancing spiritual well-being and *fostering a deep connection to the inner self.*

- **Surrounding oneself with positivity**: Exposure to uplifting environments, supportive relationships, and constructive feedback bolsters self-esteem and spiritual orientation, counteracting the effects of ***negativity and criticism***.

- **Balancing material and spiritual pursuits**: Prioritizing inner growth, ethical living, and long-term fulfilment over ***immediate sensory pleasures and material wealth*** fosters a profound connection to one's divine nature.

- **Embracing forgiveness and self-compassion: Letting go of guilt and shame**, and striving for spiritual harmony, rebuilds spiritual integrity and strengthens the sense of divine connection.

Chapter 3

Ayodhya, Lanka, Kishkindha

Ayodhya, the capital of the Kosala kingdom, is depicted in the Valmiki Ramayana as an ancient and prosperous city. It is situated on the banks of the Sarayu River and is renowned for its grandeur, wealth, and spiritual significance. The city is described as beautifully planned, with wide streets, splendid palaces, and lush gardens. The citizens of Ayodhya are portrayed as virtuous, learned, and happy, living under the just and benevolent rule of King Dasharatha. Ayodhya serves as the starting point of the epic and symbolizes the ideal kingdom, embodying the principles of dharma (righteousness), peace, and prosperity. It is also the birthplace of Lord Rama, the hero of the Ramayana, and is central to many significant events in the epic.

Lanka, the kingdom ruled by the rakshasa king Ravana, is described in the Valmiki Ramayana as a magnificent and fortified island city. It is situated on the southern tip of the Indian subcontinent, surrounded by the sea. Lanka is characterized by its immense wealth, architectural splendour, and advanced infrastructure. The city is filled with golden palaces, intricate carvings, and beautiful gardens. Despite its beauty, Lanka is also depicted as a place of moral corruption and indulgence, ruled by Ravana's tyranny. The abduction of Sita and her imprisonment in the Ashoka Vatika Garden in Lanka are central to the epic's conflict. Lanka symbolizes the dark forces that must be overcome to restore dharma and righteousness.

Kishkindha is the kingdom of the Vanaras (forest dwelling monkey like beings) and is described in the Valmiki Ramayana as a forested and mountainous region. It is located near the Pampa (Tungabhadra) River and is known for its natural beauty, with dense forests, caves, and waterfalls. Kishkindha is ruled by the Vanara king Sugriva, who becomes an ally of Rama in his quest to rescue Sita. The kingdom plays a crucial role in the epic, as it is here that Rama meets Hanuman and forms an alliance with Sugriva. The Vanaras of Kishkindha, led by Hanuman, are instrumental in locating Sita and assisting Rama in his battle against Ravana. Kishkindha represents loyalty, courage, and the power of friendship and alliances in overcoming adversity.

These three regions—Ayodhya, Lanka, and Kishkindha—serve as the primary settings for the key events in the Valmiki Ramayana, each embodying distinct aspects of the epic's themes and narrative.

The Ramayana concludes with Rama's continued rule over Ayodhya, epitomizing the ideals of justice, righteousness, and compassion.

Throughout the epic, Hanuman, the devoted servant of Rama, plays a pivotal role. His loyalty, strength, and devotion make him a crucial figure in the rescue of Sita and the defeat of Ravana, embodying the virtues of selfless service and unwavering faith.

Delving Deeper....

In the Valmiki Ramayana, Ayodhya can be interpreted as the city ruled by divine beings, symbolizing the inner kingdom within each one of us that represents the ideal state of consciousness and spiritual harmony. It is in Ayodhya that Lord Rama and his divine siblings are born. Rama embodies dharma (righteousness) and the inner divine nature, destined to overcome the harm caused by Ravana. Ravana, the Rakshasa king of Lanka, symbolizes profane tendencies, self- indulgence, and egotism that hinder the pursuit of divine evolution. Ayodhya, therefore, stands as a symbol of the being's purest aspirations and its potential for divine realization.

Kishkindha is the land of the Vanaras—described as forest dwellers and monkey-like beings—represent the mind's dynamic, untamed aspects. In this interpretation, the Vanaras symbolize the mental faculties of human beings that, when aligned with divine purpose, can aid in overcoming the profane, sensory cravings, and egoistic tendencies personified by Ravana.

The Alliance with Kishkindha Vanaras under the leadership of Sugriva and the unwavering devotion of Hanuman, illustrates the mind's potential to support the inner divine forces. Hanuman represents the power of focused, disciplined devotion in serving the divine purpose, exemplifying how the mind, when harnessed correctly, can be a powerful ally in the journey towards spiritual growth and enlightenment.

Who are Vanaras?

The Vanaras in the Ramayana can indeed be seen as representing different aspects of the human mind, each with distinct characteristic and play various roles in the journey toward spiritual realization.

Forest-Dwelling Vanaras: These beings, depicted as monkey-like reside in forest, symbolize the thoughts that jump around in the human mind. Their restless nature and constant movement mirror how our thoughts often scatter, exploring and reacting to various stimuli. In this interpretation we assume that they are the thoughts in our mind.

Three Key Aspects of the Mind

Hanuman – The Devotional Mind

Hanuman represents the devotional aspect of the mind, characterized by unwavering faith, loyalty, and dedication. This aspect of the mind is powerful because it is aligned with the divine purpose and supports the quest of spiritual evolution. Hanuman's devotion to Rama illustrates how this part of the mind can lead us toward spiritual growth and enlightenment through selfless service and focused discipline.

Sugriva – The Emotional Mind

Sugriva, the Vanara king, embodies the emotional aspect of the mind. He is driven by emotions such as fear, friendship, loyalty, and ambition. This part of the mind can be beneficial when in harmony with the higher purpose but can also be vulnerable to external influences and internal conflicts. Sugriva's journey from fear and insecurity to becoming a loyal ally of Rama reflects the potential for emotional balance and alignment with the divine will.

Vali – The Instinctive Mind

Vali, Sugriva's brother, symbolizes the instinctive and primal aspect of the mind. He is powerful and often acts on impulse and instinct, driven by physical strength and immediate gratification. This aspect of the mind can be destructive if not controlled, as it focuses on dominance, competition, and self-preservation. The conflict between Vali and Sugriva represents the struggle within the mind to balance instinctive impulses with emotional intelligence and divine devotion.

Vali is depicted as having a divine necklace that was gifted to him by Indra, the king of the gods. This necklace had magical properties—it not only enhanced Vali's strength but also allowed him to absorb half the strength of any opponent he faced in battle. Because of this, Vali was considered nearly invincible. This magical necklace plays a crucial role in understanding why Vali was so feared and why his brother Sugriva, despite his own strength, could never defeat him in battle.

Balancing Act: Navigating Mental Equilibrium

In the Ramayana, the Vanaras, depicted with tails, showcase an intriguing aspect of balance, a crucial theme that resonates deeply with the mental and emotional challenges we face. The tail, in this imaginative portrayal by Valmiki, is more than just a physical appendage; it symbolizes the grounding practices that stabilize us. Just as a tail helps the Vanaras maintain physical balance, enabling agile leaps and fluid movements, so too can mental and spiritual disciplines help us maintain psychological equilibrium.

This tail metaphor can be seen as representing various grounding practices like mindfulness, meditation, or other forms of spiritual discipline that anchor the mind. These practices are vital in helping individuals find a sense of balance amidst the constant jumping of thoughts—the mental leaps from fear to joy, from anxiety to hope, which characterize the human experience. Just as the Vanaras use their tails to expertly navigate the branches of trees, these grounding practices help us navigate life's ups and downs, providing stability in the face of life's metaphorical winds and storms.

Valmiki's poetic depiction invites readers to consider how their own "tails," or stabilizing practices, support their journey through life's complexities. It encourages a reflective look at how we manage our mental and emotional poise amidst the chaotic jumps of our daily thoughts and feelings. Through this lens, the Vanaras not only symbolize freedom and agility but also the wise management of that freedom through self-regulation and mindful balance.

Sage Valmiki's Poetic Creativity

Valmiki's portrayal of the Vanaras in his epic, describing them as monkey-like forest dwellers, reflects a profound conceptualization of the human mind's dynamic and exploratory nature. The Vanaras, embodying agility, curiosity, and a primal connection to nature, symbolize the untamed aspects of the mind. Much like the forest they inhabit, the Vanaras represent the uncharted territories of human consciousness, where thoughts and emotions roam freely, leaping from one idea to another in search of understanding and significance.

The forest setting serves as a metaphor for the mind's natural state, often chaotic yet rich with potential for discovery and growth. Just as the Vanaras traverse through dense foliage and diverse landscapes, the human mind navigates through the complexities of thoughts, desires, and challenges. Valmiki's poetic creativity lies in depicting these characters not merely as physical beings but as embodiments of psychological traits and states of mind.

Through this imaginative portrayal, Valmiki invites readers to contemplate the parallels between the external world of the epic and the internal landscape of the human psyche. The Vanaras' adventures and interactions mirror the cognitive and emotional journeys individuals undertake in their quest for self-discovery and purpose. Thus, Valmiki's depiction of the Vanaras transcends mere description, offering a profound exploration of human psychology and the complexities of inner life through the lens of epic storytelling.

Hanuman's Dominance

Among the Vanaras, Hanuman stands out as the most powerful because the devotional mind, when harnessed, can overcome all other aspects. His strength, dedication, and unwavering focus on Rama represent the ultimate potential of the mind when directed toward spiritual devotion and divine alignment.

In summary, the forest-dwelling Vanaras in the Ramayana symbolize the various facets of the human mind. Through the characters of Hanuman, Sugriva, and Vali, Valmiki poetically captures the inner workings of our thoughts and emotions. Among them, Hanuman, the devotional mind, is the most powerful, guiding us towards balance, spiritual resilience, and the realization of our divine nature.

Who are Rakshasas?

In the epic Ramayana, rakshasas are not merely demonic creatures; they symbolize the destructive tendencies that disrupt spiritual growth and moral order. Unlike Western traditions where evil is often a distinct external force, in Hindu thought, such negativity is seen as ignorance—a lack of spiritual awareness that can be transformed. These beings in the narrative frequently assail sages in the forest, obstructing their sacred rituals, or yagnas, which are vital for maintaining cosmic balance and advancing spiritual evolution. Yagnas, involving offerings into a sacred fire accompanied by mantras, range from daily purifications like Agnihotra to grand royal ceremonies like the Ashvamedha Yagna. Their goal is to purify the participants and environment, thereby fostering spiritual and communal harmony.

Lord Rama's incarnation is deeply tied to protecting these sages from the malevolence of rakshasas, especially under the tyranny of Ravana. His defence of these holy men not only exemplifies his commitment to dharma but also ensures the continuation of their yagnas, critical for sustaining the spiritual fabric of the world. Figures like Vishwamitra specifically sought Rama's protection, underscoring the significance of his divine mission. Rama's conquests over such adversaries safeguard the sanctity of spiritual practices, asserting that righteousness will prevail.

Today, rakshasas can be seen as metaphors for the challenges we face on our spiritual journeys—excessive materialism, unchecked ego, overwhelming greed, and disruptive emotions like anger and fear. These negative forces act as barriers to our inner peace and spiritual enlightenment. Overcoming them requires a conscious effort to cultivate mindfulness, self-discipline, and a profound understanding of spiritual principles. Through this process, we can achieve a state of personal growth and harmony, echoing the triumphs of Rama over his shadowy foes.

In the Valmiki Ramayana some prominent rakshasas are:

Ravana:

Hedonistic and Egotistic: Ravana represents the personification of false prestige and egotism. He indulges in sensory pleasures without discrimination and is driven by his insatiable desires, particularly for power and dominance.

Usurper: Ravana's tendency to usurp—be it land, wealth, or personal relationships—highlights his blatant disregard for ethical boundaries and fairness. His actions consistently demonstrate a readiness to manipulate and exploit others to amass power and fulfil his desires. This character trait underscores his role as an antagonist in the epic, who prioritizes personal ambition over moral and rightful conduct.

Kumbhakarna:

Pangs of Hunger: Kumbhakarna epitomizes the insatiable appetite for sensory pleasures. His legendary slumber and periods of awakening primarily for eating illustrate an extreme level of indulgence, showcasing the struggle to regulate primal desires.

Complex Discernment: While Kumbhakarna's actions initially seem driven by primal instincts, a deeper look reveals a nuanced understanding of moral and ethical stakes. His initial counsel to Ravana against abducting Sita reflects his capacity for rational thought and moral reasoning, even though he ultimately succumbs to familial loyalty and the dictates of his brother. This portrays Kumbhakarna not merely as lacking discernment but as a figure caught between his moral convictions and his obligations, highlighting the complexity of his character in the epic narrative.

Khara

Abusive Words: Khara is characterized by his abusive and harsh speech. He uses language as a weapon to intimidate and belittle others, reflecting an aggressive and hostile nature.

Lack of Respect: His disrespectful behaviour towards others signifies a lack of empathy and compassion, focusing instead on asserting dominance through verbal aggression.

Dushana:

Abusive Talk: Like Khara, Dushana also engages in offensive speech and aggressive behaviour. He supports Khara in his antagonistic actions, embodying a lack of moral restraint and ethical conduct.

Aggression: His role as a follower of Khara underscores his willingness to participate in acts of violence and intimidation, further illustrating the destructive tendencies associated with rakshasas.

Shurpanakha:

Covetousness and Usurpation: Shurpanakha is characterized by her covetous nature and desire to possess what belongs to others, particularly her attraction towards Rama and later, Lakshman.

Manipulative: She manipulates situations and individuals to fulfil her desires, disregarding the consequences of her actions and the impact on others.

Indrajit:

Feeling of Invincibility: Due to the ability to overcome some aspects of Nature, he is a master of illusion and have many creative tools that prove to be the true strength of Lanka.

Master of Illusion: Renowned as a master of illusion, skilfully using his magical abilities to create complex and bewildering deceptions on the battlefield. His mastery over illusions allows him to manipulate perceptions, making him a formidable opponent who can mislead and confuse even the most skilled warriors.

Uncovering More - Rakshasas and Vanaras:

As we delve deeper into the secrets of the Ramayana, further exploration will unveil other rakshasas like Maricha (representing deception and destructive tendencies), Subahu (symbolizing unchecked lust), many others who personify various negative traits and challenges encountered on the spiritual path. These figures serve as allegorical mirrors, reflecting the inner struggles and external obstacles that individuals must confront in their quest for spiritual evolution and self-mastery.

Can a Rakshasa transform?

Rakshasas in the Ramayana are often portrayed with a complexity that allows for transformation and redemption. The story of Vibhishana exemplifies this potential for change. Despite being Ravana's brother, Vibhishana recognizes the righteousness of Rama and the moral failings of Ravana's actions, choosing to align himself with dharma by defecting to Rama's side. This decision highlights that even among Rakshasas, there is the capacity for discerning right from wrong and making choices that lead to spiritual growth.

The reluctance of other Rakshasas to abandon Ravana, despite their awareness of his wrongdoings, illustrates a range of motivations and loyalties. Many may have been bound by familial ties, fear of Ravana's power, or the inertia of their own moral choices. However, their stories serve as a reminder that transformation is available to all beings, regardless of their origins or past actions. It is the recognition of divine compassion and the conscious choice to embrace it that marks the path to redemption. Those who resist such transformation and cling to their destructive ways ultimately face their downfall, as seen in the fates of die-hard characters like Ravana and Indrajit. This narrative underscores the universal possibility of change and redemption, even for a Rakshasa.

Similarly, the Vanaras, represented prominently by Hanuman, Sugriva, and Vali, embody positive mental qualities like devotion, loyalty, courage, and disciplined action, which assist in overcoming the rakshasas and aligning with higher spiritual values. The Vanaras also live in forest.

The forest plays a crucial role in Rama's journey in the Ramayana. It serves as a transformative setting where Rama encounters sages, learns about dharma, and befriends the Vanaras led by Sugriva and Hanuman. These allies assist him in facing challenges and defeating many rakshasas. The forest symbolizes a place where Rama's virtues are tested, preparing him for his ultimate battle against Ravana in Lanka. It highlights the interplay between spiritual growth and external conflicts in Rama's epic tale and in a way all of us ... We spend much of our lives searching through the forest of life, seeking meaning and direction.

Angad

Another important Vanara is Angad, the son of Vali and a prominent figure in the Ramayana. He was chosen as the chief of the Vanara army for several compelling reasons. Firstly, he inherited his father's strength and courage, making him a formidable warrior among the Vanaras. His lineage as Vali's son also bestowed upon him a natural leadership role within the Vanara community.

Angad, allegorically, as the progeny of the Instinctive Mind (Vali) plays an important role due to his inherent abilities.

Symbol of Strength and Willpower: Angad is known for his physical prowess and determination, traits inherited from his father Vali. This strength symbolizes the primal instincts within the human mind that are geared towards defence, survival, and asserting dominance when faced with adversity, harm.

Combativeness and Readiness to Oppose: Like his father Vali, Angad exemplifies a readiness to confront and oppose obstacles. This trait mirrors the instinctive response of the mind to defend itself against threats or challenges, whether internal (emotional) or external (physical or environmental).

Impulsivity and Assertiveness: Angad's actions often reflect impulsivity and assertiveness, characteristics typical of the instinctive mind. This aspect of the mind operates on immediate reactions and responses, driven by survival instincts and the need to secure one's position or territory.

Alignment with Survival Instincts: In the context of the Ramayana, Angad's role in the battle against Ravana's forces underscores his instinctive drive to protect and preserve. His loyalty to Rama and dedication to the cause of righteousness highlight how the instinctive mind can align with higher values when directed towards a noble purpose.

Balancing Act with Higher Qualities: While Angad represents the instinctive mind's readiness for combat with the opposition, his character also evolves through loyalty, discipline, and alignment to Dharma. This evolution suggests that the instinctive mind, when guided by higher virtues and wisdom, can contribute positively to spiritual growth and moral integrity.

In summary, Angad in the Ramayana symbolizes the instinctive aspect of the human mind that is combative, ready to oppose challenges, and driven by survival instincts. His character serves a reminder of the need to harness and balance this instinctive energy with higher qualities such as loyalty, discipline, and alignment with divine principles, ultimately contributing to inner strength and spiritual evolution.

Lanka, ruled by Ravana, epitomizes the realm of materialism, sensual indulgence, and moral corruption. It is the stronghold of egoistic and self-gratification tendencies that disrupt spiritual harmony and righteousness.

The abduction of Sita and her imprisonment in Lanka represent the captivity of faith and virtue by these darker forces. The battle to rescue Sita from Lanka symbolizes the spiritual struggle to reclaim our divine nature from the clutches of material and ego-driven desires.

The ultimate triumph of Rama over Ravana and the establishment of Rama Rajya signifies the restoration of a just, moral, and ideal state of being. Rama Rajya is the epitome of a society, and an individual life governed by dharma, compassion, and righteousness. It is the realization of the divine potential within each person, where the profane tendencies are subdued, and the divine qualities reign supreme.

Through this allegorical interpretation, Ayodhya, Lanka, and Kishkindha offer profound insights into the human psyche. Ayodhya represents the divine potential within us, Kishkindha symbolizes the mind's role in the spiritual journey, and Lanka illustrates the challenges posed by material and egoistic desires. Together, these realms depict the eternal struggle within us and guide us towards spiritual growth, enlightenment, and the establishment of an ideal, divinely aligned life.

Aligning the Mind with Spiritual Purpose

In the Ramayana, the Vanaras (thoughts) align with a higher spiritual quest during their mission to find Sita, symbolizing the mind's dedication to a divine cause.

This pivotal commitment showcases their transformation, utilizing their inherent traits—exploration, strength, and loyalty—for a noble purpose.

It illustrates that when directed by virtues like devotion and righteousness, the thoughts in the mind can transcend its limitations and achieve significant spiritual and personal growth.

This commitment to a higher goal, guided by a leader embodying spiritual value, highlights the potential for profound internal transformation and the realization of one's spiritual potential.

Five Self-Reflection questions

3.1 Can you identify these

1. Ayodhya - an inner spiritual kingdom within you, where all your inherent divine qualities reside?

2. Lanka – an inner egoistic hedonistic sensory kingdom within you, where your inherent profane side, which potentially masks your divine nature reside and is ruled by Ravana?

3. Kishkindha – the untamed and natural state of the mind (a kingdom), filled with emotions and thoughts that leap and scatter, searching for meaning and purpose?

At this point in your life which Kingdom dominates?

Explanatory note:

Mental states (Kishkindha) and sensory-driven cravings (Lanka) are distinct aspects of human experience. Mental states, like happiness, sadness, calmness, and devotion arise from internal cognitive processes and emotional experiences, shaping long-term behaviour and overall well-being. In contrast, sensory-driven cravings, such as desires for food, comfort, or physical pleasure, are triggered by external stimuli and focus on immediate gratification. While mental states can be regulated through mindfulness, sensory-driven cravings require conscious effort to control. Understanding these differences helps us balance immediate desires with deeper emotional well-being.

3.2 Can you relate to the analogy of a monkey's tail to the mind's quest for balance?

Self-reflect - How balanced are you?

Explanatory note:

Just as a monkey uses its tail to navigate and maintain balance while swinging through trees, our minds strive to find equilibrium amidst the chaos of thoughts and emotions. The monkey's agile and adaptive movements mirror the mind's flexibility and ability to adjust to changing circumstances. Similarly, the mind, like the monkey, requires balance to navigate through life's challenges and maintain inner harmony. This metaphor highlights the importance of mindfulness and mental agility in achieving a balanced state of being.

3.3 In a modern context, can you relate to the following practices that can align your mental state and aid in your pursuit of divine realization, akin to the Vanara army aligning with Rama in their quest to regain Sita?

(Being part of the Vanara army in modern life is to adopt practices as explained below)

Explanatory Note

- Vanaras aligned their energies in support of Rama's mission (mindfulness)

- Vanaras reflected on their roles and strengths in aiding Rama (self- reflection)

- Vanaras aligned with Rama's righteous cause (aligning with the divine purpose)

- Vanaras' dedication and loyalty to Rama's mission of righteousness and justice (service and compassion)

- Vanaras displayed emotional balance through positive relationships, emotional intelligence, and inner harmony and resilience

- Vanaras maintained faith and optimism in their quest along with Rama.

3.4 Reflect on character of Angad his qualities that made him the commander of the Vanara army as below,

Reflect your own abilities

- Courage and Determination: Angad's bravery and determination were critical in facing challenging situations.

- Resilience: He displayed the ability to endure hardships and remain committed to his goals.

- Unity: Angad was adept at fostering cohesion within his diverse group.

- Strategic Thinking: He skilfully exploited the weaknesses of adversaries while maximizing his group's strengths.

- Physical Prowess: Known for his strength and agility, Angad effectively navigated through physical challenges.

- Devotion and Commitment: His profound dedication to Rama and the mission motivated and inspired his troops, contributing to their success.

Consider how you can cultivate and apply these qualities in your personal and professional life to overcome challenges and lead effectively.

3.5 Can you relate to the ten heads of Ravana as an analogy and each head represents a distinct negative trait.

Self-reflect your own control of these?

1. Lust - An insatiable desire for physical pleasures that distracts from spiritual pursuits.

2. Greed - An excessive craving for material wealth and possessions, that leads to moral corruption.

3. Pride - An inflated sense of self-importance that blinds one to own flaws and the needs of others.

4. Anger - Uncontrolled rage that causes harm and alienates others.

5. Delusion - A state of confusion or misunderstanding that prevents clear thinking and wisdom.

6. Envy - A deep-seated jealousy that breeds resentment and disrupts harmony.

7. Gluttony - Overindulgence in food and drink, symbolizing a lack of self-control.

8. Sloth - Laziness and an aversion to effort, hindering personal and spiritual growth.

9. Hatred - Intense dislike that fosters negativity and conflict.

10. Attachment - Clinging to people, things, or ideas that prevents detachment and spiritual liberation.

List down actions...... you will take to keep these in check

Chapter 4

The Quest of Vishwamitra and Wedding With Sita

4.1 Overview

The tranquil life in Ayodhya takes a turn when Sage Vishwamitra arrives, seeking help to protect his yagna (sacrificial ritual) from disruptive demons, particularly Tataka, Maricha and Subahu. Despite his initial hesitation, King Dasharatha, understanding the higher purpose, agrees to send Rama and Lakshman with the sage.

Under Vishwamitra's guidance, Rama demonstrates his strength and righteousness by defeating the ferocious Tataka, Maricha and Subahu, cleansing the forest of their terror. This journey serves as a rite of passage, showcasing Rama's divine mission and his readiness to uphold dharma.

Vishwamitra then leads the brothers to the kingdom of Mithila, ruled by King Janaka, who is holding a marriage challenge for his daughter, Sita. The challenge is to string the divine bow of Shiva, an almost impossible feat. Rama, with his divine prowess, not only strings the bow but also breaks it, winning Sita's hand in marriage. This event symbolizes the union of two divine souls, with Sita being an incarnation of Lakshmi.

The marriage celebrations extend as Rama's brothers also find their matches in Sita's sisters. Lakshman marries Urmila, Bharata marries Mandavi, and Shatrughna weds Shrutakirti. These unions further solidify the bonds between the kingdoms of Ayodhya and Mithila.

The BalaKanda concludes with the joyous return of the princes and their brides to Ayodhya, marking the beginning of a new era, setting the stage for the epic adventures and profound lessons that follow in the Ramayana.

Delving Deeper....

At the heart of this epic stands Lord Rama, the personification of Vishnu, the Preserver. Rama embodies the ultimate righteousness, duty, and compassion. His divine nature and unwavering commitment to dharma (righteousness) serve as a guiding light for all, illuminating the path of virtue and justice. As Vishnu's incarnation, Rama's presence on Earth is to restore balance and harmony, confronting and overcoming the forces of darkness and adharma (unrighteousness).

Lakshman, Rama's loyal brother, personifies the **ability to stay focused and move ahead on life's journey**. His unwavering devotion to Rama is matched by his intense concentration and determination. Lakshman's steadfastness and single-minded pursuit of duty symbolize the focused mind, always ready to protect and serve the higher purpose. His character teaches us the importance of dedication, discipline, and perseverance in achieving our goals and fulfilling our responsibilities.

Bharata, another beloved brother of Rama, represents the **ability to bear the burden with grace and fortitude**. His profound sense of duty and loyalty to his family is unparalleled. Despite being given the throne of Ayodhya in Rama's absence, Bharata chooses to rule as a caretaker, placing Rama's sandals on the throne as a symbol of his true king. Bharata's character epitomizes selflessness, sacrifice, and the strength to carry heavy responsibilities while remaining humble and devoted to a higher cause.

Shatrughna, the youngest brother, embodies the tone of **amicability and the quality of being without enemies**. His gentle nature and harmonious disposition make him a beloved figure among his family and subjects. Shatrughna's ability to foster peace and goodwill highlights the importance of maintaining harmony and building positive relationships. His character reflects the ideal of living a life free from conflict, embracing compassion, and nurturing friendships.

There are not many references of Shatrughna the youngest of the four brothers. He dedicated himself in the service of his brother, Bharata. When Bharata, decided to stay at Nandigram, Shatrughna wanted to accompany him. But on his brother's request, he stayed in Ayodhya and looked after the state as an administrator. Shatrughna, the youngest, became the sole comfort for the three queen mothers during the time when Rama, Lakshman, and Bharata were away from Ayodhya.

Shatrughna played a relatively minor role in the Ramayana war but was important to the main story and goal of the epic since he managed Ayodhya. His chief exploit was the killing of Lavanasura, the demon King of Madhupura (Mathura) who was a nephew of Ravana, the King of Lanka, slain by Rama as narrated in the last Uttara Kanda.

Together, these four brothers represent a complete spectrum of virtues essential for a balanced and fulfilling life. Rama's divine righteousness, Lakshman's focused determination,

Bharata's selfless duty, and Shatrughna's harmonious nature combine to create a powerful narrative of human potential and spiritual growth. Their lives and actions teach us that by embodying these qualities, we can navigate the complexities of life, overcome challenges, and strive toward our higher nature.

4.1 In the service of Vishwamitra

In the Bala Kanda of the Valmiki Ramayana, Sage Vishwamitra approaches King Dasharatha to request the help of his sons, Rama and Lakshman, to protect his yajna (sacrifice) from disruptive rakshasas (demons). Reluctantly, Dasharatha agrees, and the young princes set off with Vishwamitra, traversing dense, mystical forests and sacred rivers. Along the way, Vishwamitra imparts divine knowledge and celestial weaponry to Rama. Their first significant encounter is with the demoness Tataka, whom Rama slays, restoring peace to the forest. They then reach Vishwamitra's ashram, where the rakshasas Maricha and Subahu attempt to disrupt the sacrifice. Rama uses a powerful celestial arrow to send Maricha flying across the ocean and kills Subahu, ensuring the successful completion of the yajna. Their journey through varied landscapes, filled with holy sites and hermitages, demonstrates their bravery and commitment to dharma, setting the stage for the larger events of the Ramayana.

Delving Deeper....

This is the first time that Rama meets Rakshasas'. Tataka is a human flesh-eating variety possibly a cannibal and so the first rakshasi that Rama eliminates is the cannibalistic tendency prevalent in the past, a prerequisite to be eliminated to propagate human evolution, after that two other rakshasas are Maricha and Subahu who prevented the sages from completing their yagnas

The two rakshasas were Maricha and Subahu, Maricha (representing killing and destructive tendencies), Subahu (symbolizing unchecked carnal lust) both animalistic tendencies, they cause significant disruptions by desecrating sacred rituals and spreading fear. They frequently showered blood, flesh, and bones on sacrificial fires, making it impossible for the sages to complete their yajnas. Their actions created an atmosphere of fear and chaos, obstructing the sages' meditative and spiritual practices. By corrupting the environment, they turned the peaceful forest into a place of turmoil. Rama, accompanied by Lakshman and Sage Vishwamitra, eliminated Maricha and Subahu and earlier Tataka, restoring the sanctity of the sages' rituals and allowing them to maintain the spiritual and cosmic balance and enable the evolution of human beings into higher consciousness.

4.2 Ahalya Moksha – redemption

As Rama and Lakshman journey with Sage Vishwamitra, they arrive at the ashram of Sage Gautama. Vishwamitra narrates the tale of Ahalya, Sage Gautama's wife, who had been cursed by her husband for her infidelity with Indra. However, in Valmiki Ramayana the curse did not turn her into a stone. Instead, she was rendered invisible and condemned to live in isolation, subsisting only on air, with her penance as her only companion. Vishwamitra tells Rama that Ahalya will be redeemed by his touch.

Rama enters the ashram, and as soon as he steps in, Ahalya emerges from her invisible state, shining with a divine radiance. Upon seeing Rama, she regains her physical form and welcomes him with reverence. Rama's presence and his touch bring an end to her curse. Sage Gautama appears, acknowledges the divine intervention, and forgives Ahalya, welcoming her back. Ahalya, now redeemed, offers her gratitude to Rama and resumes her place beside her husband. This act of redemption highlights Rama's role as a divine being capable of alleviating suffering and restoring goodness.

This story symbolizes the power of divine grace and the importance of penance, repentance, and forgiveness in achieving redemption.

Delving Deeper....

The episode of Ahalya in the Ramayana, situated between the elimination of the rakshasas Tataka, Subahu and Rama's wedding to Sita, serves as a profound metaphor. Ahalya's infidelity, driven by the urges of nature, led her to a life of invisibility to divinity, symbolizing a state of being disconnected from spiritual awareness. However, the very presence of Rama, representing divine grace, brings her redemption. This underscores the transformative power of divine intervention, illustrating that even when individuals succumb to their baser instincts, they can be redeemed through sincere repentance and the grace of the divine.

The story of Ahalya shows that, despite mistakes and lapses in ignorance (symbolized by her infidelity with Indra), divine grace remains accessible. Rama's arrival and Ahalya's subsequent redemption signify the idea that the divine presence in the mortal world can dispel sin and the negative consequences of ignorance, offering a path to spiritual restoration. This narrative emphasizes the boundless compassion and redeeming power of divinity, encouraging humans to seek forgiveness and strive for spiritual purity, regardless of their past actions.

4.3 Sita and Rama are wedded

Sita's wedding and the breaking of the Shiva Dhanush are central to the Ramayana's narrative, symbolizing divine providence and valour. This sequence begins with King Janaka discovering Sita in a furrow while preparing a field for a sacred ritual, indicating her heavenly origins. Janaka, recognizing the significance of this miraculous event, raises Sita as his daughter in Mithila.

The Shiva Dhanush, a formidable bow gifted by Shiva, becomes integral to Sita's swayamvara (a ceremony to choose her husband), symbolizing immense physical strength and spiritual worthiness. Note in Valmiki's rendering the dramatic scene of the swayamvara is not depicted.

The challenge to string the bow, deemed unmanageable by many, is effortlessly met by Rama, who not only strings the bow but also breaks it while testing its strength. This act signifies Rama's superhuman prowess and divine nature, fulfilling Janaka's condition for Sita's hand in marriage.

The breaking of the bow seals Rama's role as a suitable consort for Sita, intertwining their fates and propelling the epic's subsequent events. This moment, underscoring Rama's credentials as both a warrior and a divinely favoured hero, sets the stage for the unfolding drama of duty, devotion, and destiny that defines their lives together.

You've reached your GPT-4o limit.

Delving Deeper....

The Shiva Dhanush (Pinaka) symbolizes several profound concepts:

- Mastery over mental faculties and sensory impulses.

- The transcendence of human limitations (breaking the impossible to string bow)

- The inspiration to reach the highest levels of spiritual awareness and overcome lower traits.

Lord Rama's breaking of the bow represents a game-changing divine gift, one that transcends human limitations and is part of a grand scheme for the evolution of human consciousness. This pivotal act signifies that such spiritual potential became accessible to all with the manifestation of Rama in human consciousness (Rama Avatar). This consciousness shift, marking a profound transformation in human potential, occurred in the Treta Yuga.

In their early quest with Vishwamitra, Rama and Lakshman had already overcome primal instincts—like cannibalism (Tataka), the desire to kill (Maricha), and uncontrolled lust (Subahu)—illustrating their control over base desires and creating the pre requisites for self- evolution.

It marks a significant moment in human history, symbolizing that with conscious effort, individuals can evolve spiritually, and achieve mastery over their inner selves.

Three Self-Reflection questions

4.1 Can you identify the presence of these traits in your inner spiritual kingdom

- **Your true self** – the eternal perfect person, one that shines the inner light (**Rama**)

- Ability to stay **focused**, being awake (**Lakshman**)

- **Bear the burden** with grace and fortitude (**Bharata**)

- **Amicability** the quality of being without enemies (**Shatrughna**)

At this point in your life which trait dominates? Are you able to connect the heroes of Ramayana as existing within everybody?

4.2 Can you relate to the concept that for spirituality to evolve, Vishwamitra caused Rama to eliminate

- Cannibalistic tendencies (Tataka)

- Killing and hostile tendencies (Maricha)

- Uncontrolled carnal behaviours (Subahu)

- Bestowed forgiveness and redemption to fallen beings (Ahalya Moksha)

Explanation: All this happened during their childhood, as Vishwamitra aimed to prepare humanity for the ability to self-evolve. He supported the divinely manifested Rama and Lakshman, to fulfil their predestined quest to eliminate rakshasa behaviour (also later in Dandakaranya) and to bestow redemption and forgiveness upon the fallen by bringing the divine into their lives (Ahalya episode)

4.3 Can the symbolic act of Rama breaking Shiva's Bow and succeeding Parashuram as an avatar be seen as a divine message that humans have the potential to evolve spiritually by overcoming personal limitations? This significant event suggests that with deliberate effort, individuals can develop divine qualities like Rama, gaining control over their thoughts and desires, which in turn advances human consciousness.

Explanatory Note

In the context of Rama breaking Shiva's Bow and thereby superseding Parashuram, the symbolism extends to the evolution of the avatars themselves, representing a shift from the warrior aspect of divinity focused on retribution (Parashuram) to one of righteousness, moral governance, and self-evolution (Rama). This transition can be seen as a metaphor for the spiritual evolution of humanity.

Chapter 5

Happenings in Ayodhya and the Aborted Coronation

Rama, the beloved prince of Ayodhya, was set to be crowned as the next king of the kingdom. However, his stepmother, Kaikeyi, intervened and demanded that her own son, Bharata, be made the king instead. Kaikeyi had previously been granted two boons by her husband, King Dasharatha, and she now cashed in on these boons to have Rama banished to the forest for 14 years in addition.

Heartbroken, King Dasharatha revealed to Rama that he must honour the boons given to Kaikeyi. Despite his father's distress, Rama gracefully accepted the decree and prepared to leave for the forest, accompanied by his wife Sita and his devoted brother Lakshman.

The people of Ayodhya were devastated by Rama's banishment, and many tried to convince him to stay. However, Rama remained resolute in his duty and dharma, unwilling to go against his father's word. On the eve of his coronation, Rama, Sita, and Lakshman set out on their journey to the forest, beginning a profound odyssey that would shape the course of the epic Ramayana.

This sudden and unjust banishment, orchestrated by Kaikeyi's political machinations, was a pivotal moment that propelled the epic narrative of the Ramayana forward, leading to Rama's heroic adventures, the abduction of Sita by the demon king Ravana, and ultimately, Rama's triumphant return to Ayodhya.

Share

Delving Deeper....

The events leading to Rama's exile in the Ramayana can be interpreted allegorically as a child's journey from divine innocence to the complexities of adolescence, where stubbornness and external influences (Kaikeyi and Manthara) overshadow one's innate divine nature. This triggers the search and eventual realization of one's life purpose.

In the serene kingdom of Ayodhya, Rama, embodies the purity and righteousness inherent in every child. His life is marked by virtue, wisdom, and a deep connection to divine dharma. However, as with every journey from childhood to adulthood, challenges too arise. It soon becomes evident that the divine Rama within, maintains equanimity in both pain and pleasure, demonstrating the resilience of the inner self.

Queen Kaikeyi, initially loving and supportive, becomes upset and falls under the sway of her maid Manthara, who symbolizes the negative influences and misguided thoughts that can sabotage an innocent mind. Manthara's insidious words represent the seeds of doubt, fear, and jealousy that can take root in a vulnerable mind, steering it away from its divine path.

Kaikeyi's unreasonable obstinacy, driven by Manthara's influence, mirrors the stubbornness that often emerges during adolescence. This stubbornness can manifest as rebelliousness, a refusal to adhere to one's inherent values, and a susceptibility to negative influences. Kaikeyi's demand for Rama's exile, motivated by her desire to secure her own son's future, reflects the ego and selfish desires that can cloud one's judgment during this tumultuous phase of life.

Rama's exile, then, becomes a metaphor for the loss of divine innocence. The pure, divine nature of the child is metaphorically "exiled" as they navigate the complexities of growing up, where external pressures and inner turmoil can obscure their inherent goodness. Just as Rama's departure from Ayodhya leads him into the wilderness, the adolescent embarks on a journey through the metaphorical wilderness of life, on a predestined quest to reclaim their divine nature.

This period of exile is crucial for growth and self-discovery. Rama's experiences in the forest, his battles with demons, and his unwavering commitment to dharma (righteousness) symbolize the trials and tribulations that an individual must face to overcome their inner darkness. Through perseverance, reflection, and adherence to higher values, one can eventually reclaim their divine essence.

Thus, the metaphor of Rama's exile serves as a powerful reminder that while the journey from childhood to adulthood is fraught with challenges, it also offers the opportunity for profound spiritual growth and the ultimate realization of one's divine potential.

5.1 King Dasharatha and Queen Kaikeyi

King Dasharatha granting boons to Kaikeyi are tied to an event during his youth. Dasharatha assisted the devas in a battle against asuras, during which Kaikeyi, his youngest wife, drove his chariot. During the battle, Dasharatha was wounded, and Kaikeyi skilfully helped him by not only driving the chariot away from the battlefield but also healing and caring for him.

It is said that Kaikeyi substituted the broken wheel of his chariot with her hand, to prevent it from collapsing. During their retreat, she also tended to Dasharatha's wounds, providing essential first aid that was crucial in preventing further harm.

This richly layered narrative often perceived as **unbelievable** is filled with symbolic meanings. King Dasharatha, whose name symbolizes his mastery over 'ten chariots,' allegorically represents the human body and psyche, steered by ten indriyas . These are categorized into Jnana Indriyas (cognitive faculties) and Karma Indriyas (action faculties), which include:

Cognitive faculties (Jnana Indriyas): Eyes (Sight), Ears (Hearing), Nose (Smell), Tongue (Taste), Skin (Touch)

Action faculties (Karma Indriyas): Hands (Handling), Feet (Movement), Vocal Cords (Speaking), Anus (Excretion), Genitals (Procreation)

Kaikeyi embodies persistence, determination, and ambition within our mind-body complex, serving as a symbol of decisiveness, determination and sometimes in extreme stubbornness.

Her role and actions during a critical battle of light over darkness (devas and asuras) where she single-handedly substituted a broken chariot wheel to save King Dasharatha, illustrate her capacity to support and compensate for weaknesses for a short duration. This act is not just about physical intervention but signifies the ability for resilience and determination during adversity.

This attribute is pivotal later in the epic when her insistence on the fulfilment of boons previously granted by Dasharatha leads to Rama's exile. This moment, driven by Kaikeyi's strong will and determination, catalyses the unfolding of key events in the Ramayana, underlining the significant influence of personal traits in shaping destinies.

While Kaikeyi is often criticized for her role in Rama's exile, a deeper analysis reveals her pivotal role in the narrative of the Ramayana. Her actions, influenced by boons granted by Dasharatha, inadvertently set the stage for key events leading to Rama's triumph and the establishment of a greater kingdom. By sending Rama into exile, Kaikeyi unknowingly positioned him to confront and defeat significant threats like Ravana, thus fulfilling his divine mission. This perspective portrays Kaikeyi's decision as a crucial catalyst in the epic, essential for the restoration of dharma and the unfolding of the divine plan, highlighting her complex role but certainly not villainous.

Chapter 6

Early Phase of Exile and Bharata's Return With Sandals

The Ayodhya Kand of the Valmiki Ramayana narrates the pivotal events from the beginning of Rama's exile to Bharata's return to Ayodhya with Rama's sandals. This section is rich in emotional depth, profound conversations, and moral dilemmas.

The Kand begins with King Dasaratha's reluctant decision to honour Queen Kaikeyi's boons, granted long ago. Influenced by Manthara, Kaikeyi demands Rama's exile for fourteen years and the coronation of her son, Bharata. Rama, embodying dharma, accepts the decree without hesitation. Sita and Lakshman insist on accompanying him, showcasing their loyalty and love.

As Rama, Sita, and Lakshman depart Ayodhya, the city is plunged into sorrow. The trio travels deep into the forest, eventually settling in Chitrakoot. The name "Chitrakoot" can be broken down into "Chitra," meaning "picture" or "beautiful," and "Koot," meaning "peak" or "hill." Symbolically, Chitrakoot represents an ideal, serene retreat away from the chaos of worldly life, where one can connect with their inner self and divine consciousness. There, they build a simple hermitage and begin their life in exile, living harmoniously with nature.

Meanwhile, Bharata, who was away during these events, returns to find Ayodhya in mourning and his father dead from grief. Shocked and dismayed by his mother's actions, Bharata refuses to accept the throne. Instead, he resolves to bring Rama back. Accompanied by ministers, soldiers, and his mothers, he journeys to Chitrakoot.

In Chitrakoot, profound conversations and debates unfold between the brothers. Bharata implores Rama to return and assume the throne, arguing that the kingdom rightfully belongs to him. Rama, however, remains steadfast in his commitment to their father's word and dharma, insisting that Bharata should rule in his stead.

These debates highlight the themes of duty, righteousness, and the complexities of familial love. Rama's adherence to dharma, despite personal loss, emphasizes his role as an exemplar of virtue. Bharata, equally noble, showcases his devotion to Rama and his own moral integrity by refusing to rule unconditionally.

In the end, Rama convinces Bharata to return to Ayodhya and rule as his regent. Bharata, deeply moved, places Rama's sandals on the throne, symbolizing powerful symbol of Ramas rightful authority, humility, devotion, and the unyielding adherence to dharma and Bharatas own temporary guardianship. He vows to live as an ascetic, awaiting Rama's return.

Thus, the Ayodhya Kand, through its narrative and dialogues, explores the profound principles of duty, sacrifice, and the pursuit of righteousness, setting the stage for the epic's subsequent events.

Delving Deeper....

In the Ramayana, Rama's exile, initiated by Kaikeyi's demands and spurred by Manthara's influence, is a profound allegory for the transition into adolescence—a pivotal time when one must leave the familiar to explore, seek purpose, and grow. This departure from Ayodhya, the divine centre of being, into the wilderness symbolizes the journey from childhood's safety into the uncertainties of life's broader experiences.

As Rama, Sita, and Lakshman settle in Chitrakoot, they engage deeply with their surroundings, mirroring the adolescent exploration of new interests and environments. This stage in the forest isn't just about survival; it's a joyful and fulfilling engagement with nature that fosters personal growth and preparation for future challenges.

Meanwhile, Bharata's role back in Ayodhya, ruling in Rama's place but keeping his sandals on the throne, represents maintaining spiritual integrity and reverence for divine principles despite physical separation from the divine essence. His leadership underscores the inner strength needed to uphold one's core values and responsibilities even when direct divine guidance seems distant.

Together, these narratives highlight the importance of both exploring new territories and maintaining a connection to one's foundational values during times of change and growth. The serene environment of Chitrakoot serves not merely as a backdrop but as an active participant in Rama and Sita's spiritual and personal development, emphasizing the critical role of nature in shaping one's journey.

6.1 – Crossing the Ganga and arrival at Chitrakoot

In the early phase of their exile, Rama, Sita, and Lakshman first arrive at the banks of the Ganga River, where they meet Guha, the tribal chieftain of the Nishadas. Guha, a loyal friend of Rama, a boatman and fisher community chief receives them with great warmth and hospitality. He offers them fruits and water and provides them with a comfortable place to rest. Understanding the gravity of their situation, Guha arranges a boat to help them cross the Ganga. He ensures the boat is cleaned and sanctified, demonstrating his deep respect and devotion to Rama. Guha himself rows the boat across the river, taking care to avoid any harm to them.

Upon crossing the Ganga, the trio continues their journey deeper into the forest. They first meet the sage Bharadwaja at his ashram near Prayag, the confluence of Ganga and Januma. Sage Bharadwaja welcomes them and provides guidance on the best path to take and advises them to proceed to Chitrakoot, a beautiful and serene forest area ideal for their stay.

Following Bharadwaja's advice, they proceed towards Chitrakoot, to cross the Ganga, Yamuna confluence they constructed a boat by themselves and along the way, encounter several other sages including Valmiki who offer their blessings and counsel. Other sages include Atri and his wife Anasuya, who play a significant role in providing spiritual and moral support. Anasuya, moved by Sita's dedication and virtues, gifts her divine garments and ornaments that would never wear out, symbolizing eternal beauty and virtue.

Upon reaching Chitrakoot, Rama, Sita, and Lakshman find solace in the picturesque surroundings. The beauty of Chitrakoot, with its lush forests, flowing streams, and abundant wildlife, offers them a peaceful haven. Rama and Sita cherish their time together, enjoying the tranquillity and natural beauty around them. They live a simple and content life, free from the burdens of the royal palace.

During their stay in Chitrakoot, news of King Dasaratha's demise reaches them with the arrival of Bharata along with the citizens of Ayodhya (see section 6.2)

Stricken with grief, Rama performs the last rites for his father at Chitrakoot, with the guidance and support of the sages in the area. This act of filial piety is significant, highlighting Rama's deep respect for his parents and his adherence to dharma (righteous duty).

Chitrakoot holds immense significance in their journey. It is not only a place of natural beauty and tranquillity but also a spiritual sanctuary where Rama, Sita, and Lakshman find peace and solace amidst their trials. The time spent in Chitrakoot strengthens their bond and prepares them for the challenges ahead. It is here that Rama's resolve to uphold dharma is fortified, and Sita and Lakshman's unwavering support becomes even more evident. The idyllic setting of Chitrakoot symbolizes a period of introspection, spiritual growth, and harmony with nature, marking an important chapter in their exile.

Delving Deeper....

This phase of the exile in the Ramayana can be interpreted allegorically as the journey of a young adult leaving home and beginning personal evolution. Crossing the Ganga symbolizes the start of this evolution, marking the transition from the familiar comfort of home to the uncertainties of the world beyond. Guha, the loyal friend and guide, represents the guide young adults associate with who impart essential skills and support to help them navigate new challenges. Guha's assistance in building the boat signifies the foundational skills and support needed to embark on their journey. It must be noted in the next river crossing at the confluence is with a boat built by the trio, skills learnt.

Along the way, Rama, Sita, and Lakshman meet various ˋsages, such as Bharadwaja, Atri, Anasuya, even Valmiki, who represent mentors and teachers guiding the young adult. These sages provide direction, wisdom, and blessings, ensuring the travellers are well-prepared for the journey ahead. This mirrors how young adults seek guidance from mentors who help shape their values and provide critical life lessons.

Eventually, they reach Chitrakoot, an idyllic location where they establish a life together in safety and beautiful surroundings. This phase can be seen as a young adult's initial establishment of independence, finding their first dwelling, and beginning to build their own life. The serene and supportive environment of Chitrakoot reflects the early stages of creating a home and finding stability and joy in new beginnings.

The unheeded calls of Bharata and even Vasistha for Rama to return to Ayodhya and the performance of Dasaratha's last rites signify a period when young adults come to terms with the pangs of missing their childhood and the eventual permanent loss of their parents to death. This represents the inevitable confrontation with loss and the acceptance of life's transient nature, underscoring the importance of honouring one's roots while continuing forward.

But life never remains still, as the young adult grows to adulthood. He must move forward seeking his purpose.

The next phase of journey from Chitrakoot to Dandakaryana signifies the ongoing journey of life, with new challenges and experiences awaiting. It reflects the continuous evolution of a young adult as they grow, learn, and face the complexities of life, ever striving to uphold their values and purpose.

6.2 Ramas advice to Bharata – managing the duties and responsibilities of daily life when separated from the core divine presence.

Lord Rama's advice to Bharata on how to govern during his period of exile provides profound guidance on conducting oneself with core values and principles, especially when separated from the core divine presence, as one might experience in adolescence.

Rama emphasizes the importance of dharma (righteousness) in governance. He advises Bharata to rule with justice, fairness, and compassion, ensuring that every decision aligns with moral and ethical standards. Rama underscores the need for humility and respect towards elders and learned advisors, highlighting the value of wisdom and experience in leadership.

Interpreted allegorically, Rama's counsel can be seen as advice for individuals on how to manage their daily lives when they feel distanced from their inner divine nature. During adolescence, a time of exploration and self-discovery, maintaining core values such as integrity, respect, and compassion is crucial. Rama's guidance suggests that even in the absence of direct divine guidance, one should act with righteousness, make decisions that reflect their true values, and seek wisdom from trusted sources.

This period of life, though seemingly disconnected from the divine, is an essential phase where adherence to core principles and ethical conduct helps navigate challenges and uncertainties, ultimately leading to personal growth and a deeper understanding of one's purpose.

6.3 Rama counters Jabali and Vasistha's' arguments – says no to immediate gratification and return to comfort zone.

In the Ramayana, when Bharata visits Rama in the forest to persuade him to return to Ayodhya, he is accompanied among others from Ayodhya also by a sage called Jabali, who presents an existential argument.

Jabali says, "Rama, life is transient. Why bind yourself to old traditions and beliefs? Enjoy the pleasures and responsibilities of today. What is the point of adhering to rigid principles in a fleeting life?"

Vashishta, the family preceptor and great sage, adds, "Rama, your place is in Ayodhya, fulfilling your royal duties. Return to the comfort and responsibilities of the throne."

However, Rama counters these arguments with a steadfast commitment to his dharma. He replies to Jabali, "Sage, ethical conduct and adherence to one's duties transcend the fleeting nature of life. True fulfilment comes from living a life of righteousness, not from immediate comforts or transient pleasures."

Turning to Vashishta, Rama respectfully says, "Great sage, I appreciate your concern, but I cannot forsake my father's command. My duty as a prince is to honour my father's wishes and uphold dharma, even if it means enduring hardships."

Interpreted allegorically, Rama's rejection of these arguments symbolizes the perseverance needed during adolescence—a period often marked by rebellion and the temptation to take the easy path. Rama's steadfastness underscores the importance of enduring hardships and staying true to one's principles, even when faced with easier, more comfortable alternatives.

This phase of adolescence is crucial, as the choices made can shape one's future. Persevering through challenges, building new alliances, listening to mentors, and continuing the search for purpose, as Rama does in the Ramayana, ultimately leads to personal growth and the discovery of one's true calling. Rama's journey is a metaphor for the transformative power of enduring hardships with integrity, leading to profound self-realization and fulfilment as the events in the rest of the epic unfold.

6.4 Paduka Pattabhisekam – the Coronation of the sandals

Bharata's decision to use Rama's sandals as a symbol of his authority in Ayodhya can be interpreted as a profound metaphor for the adolescent journey toward spiritual equanimity. When Bharata places Rama's sandals on the throne, he acknowledges Rama's rightful place and expresses his deep respect and loyalty. This act signifies his understanding that true leadership and governance must be guided by the divine principles embodied by Rama.

In the allegorical context, this decision reflects the situation where an individual, during their adolescent years, is compelled to lead a life that seeks balance and harmony, even in the absence of direct spiritual realization and committed to bear that burden. The sandals represent the divine inner self, a constant reminder of the higher values and principles that should guide one's actions.

During adolescence, individuals often face tumultuous emotions and the challenge of finding their purpose and path. Bharata's act of reverence towards Rama's sandals symbolizes the importance of staying grounded in spiritual principles, even when the direct experience of the divine seems distant. It underscores the necessity of living with humility, dedication, and an unwavering connection to one's core values.

Thus, Bharata's governance, under the symbolic presence of Rama's sandals, serves as a metaphor for maintaining a spiritual centre amidst life's challenges. It highlights the need for patience and faith, with the understanding that the return of spiritual realization is a gradual process. The spiritual centre must remain steadfast, waiting for the ultimate reunion with the divine experience, while continually supplicating to the feet of the divine (sandals), signifying ongoing devotion, humility and alignment with higher truths.

6.5 Message of Sage Atri and Anasuya

Rama, Sita, and Lakshman meet the sage Atri and his wife Anasuya during their journey while leaving Chitrakoot and deciding to proceed to the Dandakaranya forest as per the guidance of Sage Bharadwaj. Anasuya, deeply moved by Sita's dedication to Rama and her willingness to endure hardships, showers her with affection and wisdom. She praises Sita for her virtues and unwavering fidelity, bestowing upon her divine gifts—garments and ornaments that never fade or wear out, symbolizing eternal beauty and the enduring nature of virtue. Anasuya blesses Sita, enhancing her spiritual and moral strength, encouraging her to uphold dharma and fulfil her duties with unwavering faith, despite the challenges of forest life.

Meanwhile, Sage Atri blesses Rama with spiritual strength, assures him of protection in the hermitages, and encourages him to uphold righteousness with courage and integrity. This meeting underscores the importance of spiritual guidance, the power of virtue, and the support of enlightened beings in overcoming life's challenges.

Anasuya's advice on devotion, chastity, and endurance mirrors the values essential for navigating life's trials, akin to the guidance adolescents need to uphold amidst the complexities of growing up. Sage Atri's counsel emphasizes the significance of seeking wisdom and spiritual fortitude, crucial for adolescents as they face the allure of worldly temptations and adversities.

Together, these messages highlight the role of faith, resilience, and divine guidance in overcoming obstacles. They also underscore the importance of mentorship and the cultivation of virtues necessary to navigate the journey from youth to maturity. As Rama, Sita, and Lakshman continue their journey into the perilous Dandakaranya forest, encountering rakshasas and face challenges like the allure of the golden deer in Panchavati, these teachings resonate as guiding principles amidst trials and tribulations.

6.1 Are you able to conceive the Ramayana as an inner journey within us all, and the period of exile representing the transition from infancy to young childhood and later to adulthood? During this phase, children face challenges such as obstinacy, manipulation, feelings of inadequacy, and direction lessness, which can hinder them from retaining their divine nature.

Can you identify and reflect on some early childhood challenges you faced?

6.2 Can you relate the boat for crossing the Ganga, and later crossing the Ganga-Yamuna confluence, as metaphors for skill acquisition? During the first crossing, you are guided and supported by others (Guha), and later you build the boat yourself (to Chitrakoot). This signifies acquiring skills in early adolescence, helping you improvise and face situations, initially with support from others and later independently.

Can you identify and reflect on some early life skills you acquired that helped you face and overcome the challenges you encountered later?

6.3 In your early adulthood, were there any idyllic Chitrakoot-like places where you initially established your independence, found your first dwelling, and began to build your own life, took advise of mentors?

Can you jog your memory and recall the pleasant aspects of that period?

6.4 Did you believe in the instant gratification philosophy that Jabali propounded, and you led a period of life in that mode especially when you built a new comfort zone away from your childhood home?

Can you recall if that was a sustainable proposition?

6.5 Reflect on your younger adolescent days and how you faced the allure of worldly temptations and adversities?

Were you able to seek guidance, self-reflect and cultivate virtues that helped you navigate from youth to maturity?

Chapter 7

Journey to Panchavati, Surpanakha and Brothers

7.1 Journey to Panchavati

In the AranyaKanda (Book of the forest) of the Ramayana, Rama, Sita, and Lakshman journey deeper into the Dandakaranya forest, encountering various challenges also meeting sages. Their journey begins with an encounter with the demon Viradha, whom they defeat, liberating his cursed soul. This victory marks the beginning of their efforts to rid the forest of its demonic influences.

They meet several sages, including:

- Sage Sharabhanga an elderly and wise sage, offers Rama, Sita, and Lakshman his wisdom and foresight. He prophesies the great challenges that Rama will face in the future and advises him to remain steadfast in his pursuit of righteousness. After offering his blessings, Sharabhanga ascends to the heavens, having fulfilled his earthly duties.

- Sage Sutikshna, a devout ascetic, welcomes them warmly and provides them with valuable guidance. He praises Rama's dedication to dharma and offers them his blessings for their continued journey. Sutikshna's ashram provides them with a temporary sanctuary, where they can rest and rejuvenate.

- Sage Agastya: Grants Rama divine weapons, including the Brahmastra, and advises him on how to deal with the demons infesting the forest.

The trio builds their second abode in Panchavati, a beautiful and serene place filled with lush greenery and abundant wildlife, symbolizing their temporary haven amidst the harsh forest. Panchavati is located near the Godavari River, providing them with a peaceful setting to live and prepare for future challenges.

However, in the Dandakaranya forest, particularly the region of Janasthana, is known as a stronghold of Rakshasas (dark forces). This is not far from Panchavati. The presence of these malevolent beings poses constant threats to the sages and other inhabitants of the forest. The guidance from sages like Agastya proves invaluable as Rama, Sita, and Lakshman strive to protect the innocent sages involved in upliftment of society and upholding righteousness.

As they settle in Panchavati, their peace is disrupted by the arrival of Surpanakha, the rakshas whose advances towards Rama lead to a series of events culminating eventually in the abduction of Sita by Ravana. This marks the beginning of a new phase in their exile, filled with trials and the eventual battle against the strong forces of darkness. Proving eventually in the realization of their purpose.

Delving Deeper....

The experiences of Rama, Sita, and Lakshman during their exile and move to Dandakaranya can be seen as an allegory for a young adult's journey through life, moving to a new location, possibly taking up a profession, and continuing to encounter challenges while seeking guidance from wise people to prepare for facing temptations and conflicts.

The encounter with Viradha, a demon who grabs and tries to possess them, symbolizes the initial obstacles and adversaries a young adult faces when stepping into the world. These adversaries may try to take away one's possessions or peace of mind, much like how Viradha tries to capture Sita. Overcoming Viradha represents the young adult's first victory against significant challenges, instilling a sense of resilience and strength. Little do they realize that the idyllic Panchavati is near Janasthana, the place where rakshasas breed, much like a large city harbour many dark forces.

After defeating Viradha, Rama, Sita, and Lakshman meet several sages, such as Sharabhanga, Sutikshna, and Agastya. These encounters symbolize the young adult's quest for wisdom and guidance from mentors and wise individuals available in these not so safe locations. The blessings and advice from these sages equip the young adult with knowledge and spiritual strength to navigate life's complexities. Sage Agastya provides Rama with divine weapons, symbolizing the tools and skills necessary to face future adversities.

The construction of their second abode in Panchavati can be seen as the period in which the young adult moves to a city or a set up a new environment. Panchavati, despite its beauty, is surrounded by the negativity and strife of Janasthana, a stronghold of Rakshasas. This represents the challenges and negativity present in a bustling city or new workplace. However, within this environment, the young adult finds a secure and peaceful abode, symbolizing the establishment of a stable and nurturing home or personal space.

7.2 Arrival of Surpanaka and the first brush with the Rakshasa of Janastana near Panchavati

Panchavati, nestled near the demon stronghold of Janasthana, becomes a pivotal scene in the Ramayana, marked by the encounter with Surpanakha, who embodies temptation, covetousness and unchecked desire. As she provocatively attempts to lure Rama and then Lakshman, her actions spark a series of ethical challenges. The brothers' firm rejection of Surpanakha, culminating in Lakshman's drastic response to her aggression towards Sita, symbolizes a stern refusal to succumb to base impulses.

This incident triggers a violent response as Surpanakha's brothers, Khara and Dushana, symbolizing aggression and malice, launch an attack. Rama's formidable response, defeating them and their forces single-handedly, serves as a dramatic affirmation of moral and physical prowess, highlighting the victory of righteousness over malevolent forces.

The narrative escalates when a vengeful Surpanakha provokes Ravana, leading to Sita's abduction. Ravana, disturbed by the news of Rama singlehandedly routing the rakshasas in Janasthana,and misled by lust for Sita spurred by Surpanakha's tales of Sita's beauty, executes his scheme with Maricha's assistance, who transforms into a captivating golden deer to distract Rama, setting the stage for deeper conflicts and the ultimate test of virtue and valour. This sequence at Panchavati not only drives the plot forward but also deepens the thematic exploration of temptation, conflict, and ethical dilemmas that define the epic.

Delving Deeper....

Surpanakha symbolizes the temptations and covetous desires that a young adult faces, such as the desire for material possessions, power, or inappropriate relationships. Her advances and subsequent rejection by Rama and Lakshman signify the importance of resisting such temptations and maintaining integrity and focus.

The act of disfiguring Surpanakha by Lakshman represents the decisive rejection of these temptations and understanding the consequences of succumbing to them. It highlights the need for the young adult to take a firm stand against unethical or harmful desires, ensuring that these temptations do not derail their life's journey.

The battle with Khara and Dushana highlights the need to resist baser impulses and conflicts. Khara represents the hurling of curse words, while Dushana symbolizes abusive talk and creating strife. These forces are soon eliminated, signifying that as adults evolve, these tendencies are overcome.

It is at this stage that the Valmiki Ramayana introduces the Rakshasa King Ravana.

7.3 Ravana enters the story… the abduction plan

In the AranyaKanda. the narrative takes a dramatic turn with the introduction of Ravana, the Rakshasa king of Lanka. This part begins with Akampana, one of Ravana's surviving warriors from Janastana, informing Ravana about the defeat of Khara and Dushana and the destruction of all the rakshasas at Janasthana, single handedly by Rama.

Ravana, upon hearing this, is infuriated and boasts about his invincibility and power. He declares that no one has dared to challenge his might before and vows to take revenge on Rama. However, he recognizes that Rama's strength cannot be confronted directly and begins to plot a cunning plan to weaken him.

Ravana then seeks the counsel of Maricha, a powerful rakshasa who has previously encountered Rama. Initially reluctant, Maricha tries to dissuade Ravana by highlighting Rama's formidable prowess and the risks involved in confronting him. Despite Maricha's warnings, Ravana is determined and forces Maricha to comply with his plan. The plot involves Maricha transforming into a golden deer to lure Rama and Lakshman away from Sita, leaving her vulnerable.

Meanwhile, Surpanakha, still reeling from her humiliation and disfigurement by Lakshman, arrives at Ravana's court. She taunts Ravana, questioning his strength and mocking his inability to protect his own kin and territory. Her taunts and vivid description of Sita's beauty ignite Ravana's desire to possess Sita and avenge his sister's dishonour.

Ravana, spurred into action by Surpanakha's provocations and his own revengeful ambition, decides to execute his plan.

He enlists Maricha's help, and they set out for Panchavati, where Rama, Sita, and Lakshman are residing. Maricha, disguised as a golden deer, successfully captivates Sita's attention, leading Rama to pursue the deer and Lakshman to follow at Sita's behest, leaving her alone and defenceless.

This chain of events, orchestrated by Ravana's cunning and fuelled by his wrath and desire, sets the stage for the abduction of Sita, marking a pivotal moment in the Ramayana. Ravana's introduction and his subsequent actions highlight the themes of deception, ambition, and the consequences of unchecked desires.

Delving Deeper....

The Rise of Ego in Young Adulthood – The surfacing of the Ravana tendency within.

The events of AranyaKanda in the Ramayana can be seen as an metaphor for the internal conflicts that a young adult experiences. This phase of life often involves an internal rebellion, particularly when an individual feels denied or belittled in their pursuit of desires and ambitions. These experiences cause the ego to surface, pushing the individual to resort to cunning and unethical actions to establish power and assert supremacy.

In this interpretation, Ravana represents the burgeoning ego within a young adult. The defeat of Khara and Dushana, who symbolize crass and abusive tendencies, signifies the elimination of baser qualities. This marks a shift from overt aggression to more subtle and insidious forms of conflict.

When Akampana informs Ravana of the happenings at Janasthana, it is akin to a young adult becoming aware of their limitations and the threats to their sense of self. Ravana's boastfulness and subsequent plotting with Maricha symbolize the ego's determination to regain control and assert dominance by any means necessary. The ego, much like Ravana, is driven by a need to prove itself and refuses to be belittled.

Surpanakha's taunts further inflame Ravana's ego, representing external provocations that exacerbate internal insecurities and drive the individual to act out of pride and a desire for revenge. Her description of Sita's beauty can be seen as the allure of unattainable desires that fuel the ego's ambitions.

Ravana's crafting of a deceitful plan, including the manipulation of Maricha to disguise as a golden deer, signifies the ego's use of cunning and deceit to achieve its goals. The golden deer symbolizes the tempting distractions that lead one away from their true path.

When Ravana himself disguises as a sage and uses cajoling, sweet promises, and threats, it highlights how the ego can mask its true nature and employ both flattery and intimidation to manipulate and control. This period in life is marked by the ego's insistence on ruling, refusing to be undermined.

Understanding this metaphor requires a paradigm shift, recognizing that the rise of the ego and its conflicts are internal processes. Yet, intuitively, many can relate to the moments when their ego comes of age, pushing them toward actions driven by pride, desire, and the need for validation.

7.4 The abduction

In AranyaKanda, the events take a dramatic turn with the arrival of Maricha and Ravana, setting the stage for the abduction of Sita. Maricha, under Ravana's command, transforms into a golden deer to lure Rama and Lakshman away from their abode in Panchavati. Sita, captivated by the beauty of the deer, requests Rama to capture it for her. Rama, despite sensing something amiss, pursues the deer, instructing Lakshman to stay and protect Sita.

As Rama chases the golden deer, Maricha cunningly leads him deep into the forest. Eventually, Rama strikes the deer with an arrow, and in his dying moments, Maricha mimics Rama's voice, crying out for help. Alarmed by the cry, Sita urges Lakshman to go assist Rama. Despite Lakshman's initial reluctance, Sita, distressed and suspicious, harshly questions his intentions and loyalty, forcing him to leave in search of Rama. Contrary to popular retellings, the original Valmiki Ramayana does not mention the drawing of a protective Lakshman Rekha around Sita.

With both brothers away, Ravana seizes the opportunity. Disguised as a mendicant sage, he approaches Sita, who, unaware of his identity, extends her hospitality. Ravana, under the guise of a sage, engages Sita in conversation, subtly praising her beauty and inquiring about her life in the forest. As the conversation progresses, his true intentions are revealed when he discloses his identity and proposes that Sita abandon Rama to become his queen.

Sita, shocked and terrified, vehemently rejects Ravana's advances, declaring her unwavering devotion to Rama.

Ravana, angered by her rejection, abandons his disguise and forcefully abducts her. He lifts Sita into his flying chariot, the Pushpaka Vimana, and they take to the skies. Sita, in desperation, calls out for help and throws her jewellery to the ground, hoping it will serve as a clue for Rama and Lakshman.

As they fly over the forest, Sita's cries are heard by the vulture king Jatayu, who bravely attempts to rescue her. Despite his valiant effort, Jatayu is overpowered by Ravana and severely wounded. Ravana then continues his flight to Lanka, with Sita held captive.

This series of events marks a pivotal point in the Ramayana, highlighting themes of deception, loyalty, and the dire consequences of succumbing to temptation. Sita's abduction sets the stage for the ensuing conflict between Rama and Ravana, driving the epic forward into the search for Sita and the eventual battle to rescue her.

Delving Deeper....

The abduction of Sita can be interpreted allegorically as a time when young adults succumb to the allure of external attachments and accomplishments, symbolizing their ego abducting the faith in the inner divine nature. Sita represents the pure, untainted faith within an individual to the true inherent divine nature. The golden deer, with its mesmerizing beauty, symbolizes the allure of sensory pleasures and external desires that the ego chases after. A person becomes vulnerable, and this leads to the eventual abduction of inner faith.

When Sita harshly urges Lakshman to leave her and search for Rama, it metaphorically illustrates how vulnerable situations can lead to even one's inner faith being compromised or overtaken by ego-driven desires. This abduction moment signifies the internal conflict where faith, represented by Sita, becomes momentarily overshadowed by the ego's pursuits, despite initial reluctance

Sita's rejection of Ravana and her discomfort throughout the abduction signify that even though one's faith may be temporarily overshadowed by ego and external allurements; it remains inherently opposed to these forces and strives to return to its true essence. The ego, represented by Ravana, thrives on sensory pleasures and manipulative tactics, seeking to dominate and possess what it desires.

The narrative forward can be seen as the journey to restore alignment and reunite with their lost faith in the true divine nature. This parallels the journey of a young adult caught in the trap of ego but not fully aligned with it. Instead, they embark on a quest for meaning and purpose. The rest of the Ramayana, therefore, represents the process of self-discovery, overcoming ego, and reestablishing the connection with one's inner faith and true self.

This allegorical interpretation provides a deeper understanding of the Ramayana, emphasizing the inner journey and the struggles of maintaining integrity and devotion amidst the challenges of life. It underscores the significance of perseverance, self-reflection, and the ultimate triumph of righteousness and faith over ego and temptation.

7.5 Role of Jatayu – the bird from long ago…the friend of the ancestors

Rama, Sita, and Lakshman first encounter Jatayu during their exile in the Dandakaranya forest. Jatayu, an old and wise vulture, introduces himself and reveals his past connections with their family. He is the son of Aruna, the charioteer of the sun god Surya, and a close friend of King Dasharatha, Rama's father.

Jatayu pledges his support and protection to Rama and his family, showcasing his deep sense of loyalty and duty. This ancestral connection establishes a bond of trust and respect between them. Jatayu becomes a guardian figure for Sita during their time in the forest and helped then to settle in Panchavati.

When Ravana abducts Sita and carries her away in his chariot, Jatayu valiantly intervenes to rescue her. Despite his old age and frailty, Jatayu engages in a fierce battle with Ravana, attempting to thwart the abduction. He fights bravely, but Ravana ultimately overpowers him, severely injuring him and cutting off his wings. Jatayu's final act of resistance and sacrifice highlights his unwavering devotion to righteousness and his willingness to lay down his life to protect Sita.

Before succumbing to his injuries, Jatayu informs Rama and Lakshman of the direction in which Ravana took Sita. This critical piece of information propels Rama and Lakshman's quest to rescue her. Jatayu's selfless act and his final sacrifice deeply move Rama, who performs the last rites for Jatayu, honouring him as a noble warrior and a true friend.

Later in the story, Sampati, Jatayu's elder brother, plays a crucial role in aiding the search for Sita. Sampati, who had lost his ability to fly due to an injury while trying to protect Jatayu from the sun's scorching rays, learns about his brother's fate from Hanuman and the other Vanaras (monkey warriors). Moved by the loss of his brother and inspired by his bravery. As Sampathi could see far off places with his keen eyesight, Sampathi locate Sita in Lanka. He informs Hanuman and the Vanaras of Sita's whereabouts, providing them with the vital information needed to continue their mission.

Jatayu's encounter with Rama and his sacrifice symbolize the values of loyalty, bravery, and selflessness. Sampati's role underscores the importance of familial bonds and the power of collaboration in overcoming challenges. Together, their contribution significantly aids Rama's quest to rescue Sita and restore dharma.

Delving Deeper....

Jatayu's role in the Ramayana symbolizes the ancestral support and wisdom that guides a young adult through life's journey. Just as Jatayu aids Rama, Sita, and Lakshman with his knowledge, bravery, and sacrifice, ancestral influences in a young adult's life provide crucial direction and insights.

Jatayu's initial encounter with Rama and his family represents a deep connection to one's roots and heritage. His bond with King Dasharatha signifies the enduring influence of previous generations, offering protection and guidance. This ancestral support is powerfully demonstrated when Jatayu valiantly attempts to rescue Sita from Ravana, even at the cost of his own life. His bravery and sacrifice symbolize the values and virtues passed down from ancestors, reminding us of our moral duties and responsibilities.

When Jatayu informs Rama and Lakshman of the direction in which Ravana took Sita, it serves as a metaphor for ancestral wisdom pointing the way forward. Although Jatayu succumbs to his injuries, his guidance is invaluable in the quest to reclaim Sita, symbolizing the lasting impact of ancestral knowledge even after one's physical presence is gone.

Sampati, Jatayu's elder brother, further underscores the importance of ancestral influence. Upon learning of Jatayu's sacrifice, Sampati's grief transforms into a resolute determination to assist in the quest. With his keen eyesight, Sampati reveals that he has seen Sita being taken to Lanka, providing the Vanaras with the crucial information needed to continue their mission. This act represents the broader ancestral wisdom that not only recognizes challenges but also offers precise guidance on how to overcome them.

Together, Jatayu and Sampati embody the ancestral legacy that aids a young adult in their quest for purpose and meaning. The wisdom and sacrifices of past generations become guiding lights, illuminating the path to overcoming one's ego (Ravana) and resisting the allure of sensory pleasures. These lessons underscore that life's journey involves recognizing and conquering both internal and external challenges, with ancestral insights providing essential direction and strength.

In this allegory, conquering Ravana—the embodiment of ego and selfish desires—becomes the ultimate purpose of life. Ancestral guidance, as demonstrated by Jatayu and Sampati, helps a young adult realize this purpose and equips them with the wisdom needed to achieve it. This realization marks a significant step in the journey toward self-realization.

7.6 Rama's Lament…. beginning the search…getting the direction…

After Sita's abduction, Rama is overcome with grief and despair, lamenting his helplessness and loss. His sorrow is deep and heartfelt, reflecting the pain of being separated from his beloved wife. Rama's distress is palpable, and he feels utterly helpless in the face of this profound personal crisis.

Lakshman, ever wise and steadfast, offers Rama advice what a sage would have given. He reminds Rama of his divine nature, his duties, and the importance of remaining composed and resolute. Lakshman's words act as a source of strength and encouragement, helping Rama regain his focus and determination. He advises Rama to move forward, reminding him that they must continue their mission to find and rescue Sita.

After Jatayu's cremation, Rama and Lakshman leave Panchavati and venture deeper into the dense forest. Along their journey, they encounter the fearsome demon Kabanda, a grotesque creature with an enormous body, long arms, and no visible head—his face embedded in his chest. Kabanda attacks the brothers, stretching his massive arms to capture them. However, after a fierce battle, Rama and Lakshman manage to defeat him by severing his arms. As Kabanda lies dying, the curse that had transformed him into a demon is lifted, revealing his true form as a celestial being. Grateful for his release, Kabanda offers the brothers crucial advice. He urges them to seek out Sugriva, the exiled Vanara king, who would play a vital role in their quest to find Sita. This encounter marks a turning point in their journey, guiding them toward the next phase of their mission.

Continuing their journey, Rama and Lakshman arrive at the Matanga Ashram, where they meet the devoted Shabari. An elderly and ascetic woman, Shabari has been waiting for years to meet Rama, following her guru Matanga's instructions. She warmly welcomes them, offering them fruits and expressing her devotion. Shabari's unwavering faith and devotion deeply move Rama. The maintenance of the ashram and the sacrificial fire even when there were no inmates, reinforced the hope and resolve in Rama's heart.

With newfound composure and determination, Rama and Lakshman proceed towards the foothills of Kishkindha, the kingdom of the Vanaras. Here, at the threshold of a new phase in their journey, Rama is filled with renewed hope and resolve, ready to forge alliances and continue the quest to rescue Sita.

Delving Deeper....

The abduction of Sita can be seen allegorically as a time when young adults succumb to the allure of external attachments, causing an inner core of angst and a feeling of emptiness to overpower them. However, focus emerges, in the form of Lakshman's advice, urging them to move forward. They also receive direction and guidance from figures like Jatayu, representing wisdom from the past and the stars to support them.

As the young adult continues their journey to find true faith, the encounter with Kabanda metaphorically signifies seeing through their own bondage and realizing that to achieve self-resolve and move ahead, they must seek alliances. This is where the alliance with Sugriva and the Vanaras becomes crucial in the quest to find Sita, eventually leading to the alignment needed to pursue their true purpose and self-development.

Before forging the alliance with Sugriva, there is a significant meeting with Shabari, an elderly woman ascetic. Shabari's devotion and guidance impart hope and forbearance, illustrating the need to move forward even when faced with uncertainty and angst, not to be depressed. During these uncertain periods, the young adult learns the importance of patience and waiting with hope.

This allegory highlights when external allure and inner turmoil overpowers them, young adults must gather themselves, build patience, seek wisdom, and form alliances, reinforcing the resolve to continue their journey. This period of patience, waiting, and gradual forward movement is essential in the search for true faith and purpose, mirroring Rama's experiences.

In Valmiki Ramayana – even Rama the avatar of Vishnu become sorrowful despite all the power he has and must take the help of others to move forward.

7.1 Can you recall some early traumatic events when, like Viradha, someone took something that belonged to you as you were starting out on your own?

Can you identify and reflect on some early childhood challenges you faced?

7.2 Can you identify instances in your childhood when you experienced the desire to covet things or faced others wanting to take what was yours, (like Surpanakha's tendencies)?

How did you effectively deal with such situations to ward these off?

7.3 Can you recall the first time the equivalent of the "golden deer" appeared in your life, when you got carried away and eventually found yourself trapped for an extended period?

Looking back, can you now identify that as an "abduction" moment, realizing that you never truly belonged to the destination you reached—a temporary Ashoka Vatika?

7.4 Can you recall the role of elders who guided you with compassion when you felt lost and searching for a sense of belonging?

List these elders and mentors whose guidance helped you find your direction and try to list what was the essence of their support?

7.5 Reflect on your younger adolescent days when you faced feelings of emptiness and depression

How did you cope with this lack of focus and despondency? Were there moments, like visiting a serene place or encountering wise beings like Shabari, whose innocence and wisdom renewed your vigour and sense of purpose?

7.6 Reflect on how you embarked on your quest and became the change you wanted to see within yourself and the world around you

Reflect on the opportunities you seized to make the best out of your circumstances.

Chapter 8

Into Kishkindha – Forging Alliance With the Jumping Monkey-like Mind

8.1 Meeting Hanuman, Sugreeva, the Killing of Vali

Separated from Sita, Rama's longing and despair deepen. Despite the beauty surrounding him at Pampa Lake, with its lush greenery and vibrant blossoms, Rama is engulfed in sorrow. The serene environment, filled with the chirping of birds and the fragrance of flowers, contrasts sharply with his inner turmoil.

Upon reaching Rishyamuk Mountain, where Sugriva and his exiled Vanaras reside, Rama and Lakshman are approached by Hanuman, Sugriva's chief minister. Disguised as a Brahmin, Hanuman introduces himself with humility and reverence, inquiring about their identity and purpose, sensing their nobility and the burden of their quest.

Lakshman explains their mission to rescue Sita. Realizing the significance of their presence, Hanuman reveals his true Vanara form and offers his help. He takes

Rama and Lakshman to meet Sugriva, who, initially cautious, soon shares his troubles, particularly his conflict with his brother, Vali.

Sugriva explains how Vali exiled him and took his wife, Ruma. Moved by Sugriva's story and recognizing their mutual need for assistance, Rama forms an alliance with him. Rama agrees to help Sugriva reclaim his throne, and in return, Sugriva will assist in finding and rescuing Sita.

To prove his strength, Rama shoots an arrow through seven massive sala trees, a feat demonstrating his extraordinary capabilities. Convinced, Sugriva pledges his support.

Sugriva challenges Vali, who accepts the duel. During their fight, Rama, hiding and observing, shoots Vali with an arrow, fatally wounding him. As Vali lies dying, he reproaches Rama for attacking from hiding. Rama explains his dharma, stating that Vali had wronged Sugriva by taking his wife and kingdom, justifying the intervention.

Vali, realizing his mistakes and acknowledging Rama's righteousness, makes peace before dying. Sugriva performs the last rites for his brother, marking a significant turning point in Kishkindha. Tara, Vali's wife, does not fault Rama and later proves to be an important female power in Kishkindha, also as Angad's mother and who sacrificed her husband.

With Vali gone, Sugriva is crowned king of Kishkindha. True to his word, he orders the Vanaras to search for Sita. Hanuman, the most capable among them, is chosen to lead the search party due to his wisdom, strength, and devotion. However, this search does not commence immediately.

Note: In Ramayana Secrets, we present the Vanaras as representations of the untamed human mind—monkey-like, powerful, and jumpy. Valmiki's creative use of the tail serves to graphically illustrate how human thoughts balance themselves. Thus, this alliance between the mind and the inner divine self (Rama) symbolizes the need to engage with the mind and ultimately control the sensory, self-gratifying, egoistic and profane aspects within an individual, represented by Ravana.

Delving Deeper....

The alliance with Sugreeva symbolizes the engagement with the emotional mind, while Hanuman represents the devotional mind. For a young adult, strengthening both emotional and devotional intelligence is crucial to counter the fear-driven behaviours represented by the rakshasa nature.

The killing of Vali, who represents the instinctive mind, is essential because a mind ruled by pure instinct is unsuitable for higher pursuits and is susceptible to transgressions and impulses. Rama's act of hiding during the killing metaphorically signifies that as divine fervour increases within, the role of instinct and virility must diminish in the pursuit of a higher purpose. In our allegorical explanation, a young mind aligned emotionally and devotionally to the inner divine must overcome instinctive tendencies. However, it is noteworthy that Angad, Vali's son, and Tara, Vali's wife, remain crucial in the quest to find Sita later.

While the killing of Vali from hiding is often viewed as controversial, Valmiki's Ramayana provides a deeper understanding through Rama's own words, aligning the act with the principles of dharma.

The story of Vali Divine necklace also adds depth to the ethical debate around Rama's decision to kill Vali from hiding. Since Vali absorbed half the strength of anyone he fought, Rama's tactic of striking from a concealed position was the only feasible way to ensure Sugriva's survival and to overthrow Vali's tyranny. The necklace and its powers thus emphasize why it was impossible for Sugriva to defeat Vali directly, justifying Rama's decision to intervene. The necklace not only represented Vali's strength but also the imbalance of power, which Rama corrects by siding with Sugriva. This event teaches that true strength lies not in brute force alone but in righteous conduct and alignment with dharma.

As per the Valmiki narrative:

As Vali lay on the forest floor, his life ebbing away, he looked up at Rama with a mixture of pain, confusion, and betrayal. "Why, Rama?" he asked, his voice weak but filled with anguish. "Why did you strike me from the shadows? I have done no wrong to you. If you desired my life, you could have confronted me openly. What justice is there in this act?"

Rama, his expression calm yet solemn, approached the dying king. He knelt beside Vali and spoke with the clarity and authority of a king who understood the burden of his actions. "Vali," Rama began, "I did not kill you out of malice or hatred. My duty as a prince, a protector of Dharma, compelled me to act. You, Vali, are a powerful king, but you have strayed from the path of righteousness. You wronged your brother, Sugriva, without just cause, and you took what was not rightfully yours—his kingdom, his wife, and his honour."

Vali, struggling to grasp Rama's reasoning, responded, "But what gives you the right to intervene in our affairs? This is a matter between brothers. You had no reason to strike me from hiding like a coward."

Rama's gaze remained steady as he replied, "As a king, it is my duty to uphold Dharma, to protect the innocent, and to punish those who misuse their power. You, Vali, have committed acts of Adharma by usurping your brother's throne and mistreating him. A ruler must be held to the highest standards, and when a king abuses his power, it is the duty of another righteous king to correct that wrong. I struck you from hiding because in an open duel, your strength would have made you invincible. My duty was to restore justice, and this was the only way to do so."

Vali, though still pained by the manner of his death, began to understand the broader implications of Rama's actions. He realized that Rama was not just acting as an individual but as the upholder of cosmic law, whose actions were guided by the principles of Dharma.

With his last breaths, Vali accepted Rama's judgment. "I see now that you have acted in the name of righteousness, though it was hard for me to understand. I was blinded by my pride and anger, and in that blindness, I lost sight of what was right. Forgive me, Rama, for questioning your motives. I entrust my son, Angada, to your care, for I know now that he will be in the hands of a just and noble king."

Rama nodded, acknowledging Vali's repentance and promising to care for Angada as his own. As Vali's life slipped away, Rama's words lingered in the air, a reminder that the path of Dharma is often fraught with difficult decisions and that a king's duty is not just to his people, but to the higher moral order that governs the universe.

This encounter between Rama and Vali serves as a powerful narrative on the complexities of justice, the responsibilities of leadership, and the sometimes-harsh realities of upholding Dharma. It reminds us that righteousness is not always clear-cut, and the actions of the just may not always be easily understood, but they are ultimately guided by a higher moral law that seeks to maintain balance and order in the world.

Rama convinces Sugriva: The Esoteric Meaning

The two tasks Rama performs to convince Sugriva—piercing the seven Sal trees with a single arrow and scattering Dundubhi's skeleton with a kick—are deeply symbolic.

Piercing the trees demonstrates Rama's divine ability to cut through illusions and overcome obstacles with the power of righteousness and focused intention. Kicking Dundubhi's skeleton signifies the need to dispel past fears and doubts, clearing away remnants of old challenges to allow for renewal and progress.

These acts not only prove Rama's physical strength but also symbolize his capacity to overcome both internal and external obstacles, inspiring Sugriva and Hanuman.

8.2 Coronation of Sugreeva, the waiting and delayed start of search

After the defeat of Vali, Sugreeva is coronated as the king of Kishkindha and Angad as crown prince, with the support of Rama and the Vanaras. This marks a significant shift in the power dynamics within the kingdom and solidifies the alliance between Rama and Sugreeva.

Rama and Lakshman do not enter the city of Kishkindha since during the exile they must not enter, so

Rama and Lakshman retreat to the Prasravana Mountain for the monsoon season. They wait for the rains to end, understanding that it would be impossible to launch a search for Sita during the heavy rains. This period of waiting is marked by Rama's longing and despair as he endures the separation from Sita.

Once the monsoon season ends, Rama expected Sugreeva to initiate the search for Sita. However, Sugreeva, now engrossed in the pleasures of kingship and enjoying his newfound status, delays the efforts to fulfil his promise to Rama. His neglect and procrastination cause further distress to Rama.

Seeing Sugreeva's lack of action and sensing Rama's anguish, Lakshman becomes furious. He decides to confront Sugreeva about his failure to keep his promise. Lakshman's anger represents a moment of intense loyalty and dedication to Rama's cause.

Tara, Vali's widow and senior queen of the Vanaras, plays a crucial role in mediating between Lakshman and Sugreeva. She intervenes with wisdom and diplomacy, calming Lakshman and reminding Sugreeva of his duty to Rama. Her intervention is pivotal in refocusing Sugreeva on the mission at hand.

Moved by Tara's words and aware of his duty, Sugreeva springs into action. He mobilizes the Vanaras, assigning them various directions to search for Sita. Sugreeva's leadership and the dedication of the Vanaras mark the beginning of a comprehensive and determined effort to find Sita.

Delving Deeper....

After Sugriva's crowning, the period known as Chaturmasa, or the four-month monsoon season, commences. This time of heavy rains halts active pursuits, allowing Sugriva and his restored kingdom to focus on consolidating power and preparing for the mission to rescue Sita. Rama and Lakshman use this period of waiting to strategize and strengthen their resolve. Chaturmasa symbolizes the importance of patience, preparation, and waiting for favourable times and the right atmosphere before embarking on significant endeavours.

It teaches that success often depends on aligning our actions with the natural rhythms and cycles, ensuring that the conditions are ripe for progress. Sugreeva's initial delays reflect the distractions and procrastinations young adults may face when newfound responsibilities and pleasures take precedence over their commitments.

Lakshman's anger and Tara's intervention highlight the importance of loyalty, accountability, and wise counsel in overcoming delays and distractions.

The mobilization of the Vanaras symbolizes the concerted effort and focus needed to achieve one's goals.

The killing of Vali, representing the instinctive mind, and Sugriva's rise signify the necessity of moving beyond raw instincts toward a more conscious and purposeful existence. Rama's hidden role in Vali's death highlights the diminishing influence of instinct in favour of divine guidance and higher principles.

Overall, the Kishkindha phase illustrates the alignment of emotional and devotional intelligence, emphasizing its crucial role in overcoming challenges and progressing towards one's higher purpose.

8.3 The Search Parties and Leap of Hanuman

After being reminded of his promise and refocused on the mission, Sugreeva mobilizes his army of Vanaras to search for Sita. Rama sets the objective: to locate Sita and bring back information about her whereabouts. Sugreeva organizes the search into different teams, each led by prominent Vanara warriors, and assigns them specific regions to cover.

The Vanara army, consisting of countless numbers with extraordinary strength, agility, and loyalty, is a formidable force. Key figures in this army include:

- Hanuman: The wise and powerful devotee of Rama, known for his immense strength and unwavering devotion.

- Angad: The brave and energetic son of Vali, who brings youthful vigour to the mission.

- Jambavan: The wise and elderly bear, offering guidance and wisdom.

- Nala and Nila: Skilled engineers and builders, responsible for constructing vital infrastructure during the mission.

- Shatabali, Vinata, and Sushena: Other notable leaders, each with their own specialized skills and attributes.

Rama's alliance with Sugreeva ensures the mobilization of this strong counterforce,

- North Team: Led by Shatabali, tasked to search the northern regions.

- South Team: Led by Angad, with Hanuman and Jambavan as key members, tasked to search the southern regions.

- East Team: Led by Vinata, assigned to explore the eastern territories.

- West Team: Led by Sushena, directed to cover the western areas.

Each team is given specific instructions and detailed maps of their respective areas to ensure comprehensive coverage. Sugreeva emphasizes the importance of thoroughness and urgency in their mission.

Sugreeva sets a one-month deadline for the teams to report back with their findings. He stresses the importance of timely updates and the critical nature of their mission.

As the deadline approaches, most teams return with no significant leads or information about Sita's whereabouts. Their reports are filled with frustration and despair, as the extensive search seems to yield no results.

The South Team, led by Angad, Hanuman, and Jambavan, also faces despair. They reach the southern coast without any concrete information and feel demoralized, considering abandoning the search. However, the arrival of the wise and aged vulture,

Sampati, the brother of the fallen Jatayu, reveals that he saw Sita being taken to Lanka by Ravana. He provides crucial information about her location, reigniting hope among the Vanaras. This revelation is a turning point, transforming their despair into renewed determination.

Jambavan, the wise and elderly Vanara, counsels Hanuman, reminding him of his immense strength and capabilities. He motivates Hanuman, instilling confidence and resolve in him to undertake the daunting task of leaping across the ocean to reach Lanka.

Inspired by Jambavan's words and fuelled by the newfound information from Sampati, Hanuman gathers his resolve. He prepares himself to make the monumental leap across the ocean, symbolizing the Vanaras' unwavering determination and commitment to their mission.

Delving Deeper....

The initiation of the search and the formation of teams in the Ramayana symbolize a young adult's organized approach to tackling significant challenges or achieving important goals. Each team and their specific regions reflect the diverse strategies and life areas explored in the quest for solutions.

The one-month deadline and initial failures in locating Sita underscore the typical frustrations and challenges encountered in such endeavours. The Vanaras' despair mirrors the setbacks and discouragements often faced by young adults when results seem elusive.

Sampati's timely guidance represents the unexpected wisdom that often arrives from external or ancestral sources, offering new hope. Jambavan's role as a mentor is pivotal; his encouragement helps Hanuman realize his immense potential. This moment marks a critical turning point where a young adult, guided by mentorship, begins to recognize their true capabilities and embarks on a mission to fulfil their destiny.

Hanuman's determined leap across the ocean embodies the bold actions necessary to achieve ambitious goals. This segment of the Kishkindha Kanda transitions from despair to hope and from doubt to confidence, highlighting the importance of resilience, guidance, and steadfast determination in pursuing one's objectives.

Five Self-Reflection questions

8.1 Are you able to think that the Vanaras represent thoughts in the mind? When these thoughts are aligned emotionally and devotionally to your true nature, they harness the power to overcome ego and sensory enjoyments?

List some sensory addictions you were able to overcome through conscious effort, willpower, self-restraint, and spiritual practice.

Explanatory Note:

In this context, the Vanaras symbolize the untamed, powerful, and often erratic thoughts in the mind. When these thoughts are harmonized through emotional and devotional alignment, they can transcend the pull of the ego and sensory pleasures. This exercise encourages self-reflection on how spiritual discipline and mental fortitude have helped you conquer certain sensory temptations and egoistic tendencies

8.2 Have you ever experienced a moment of emotional maturity where you realized that your ego does not define your true self? Reflect on specific instances or triggers in your life that led to this transformative understanding.

What were the events or experiences that sparked this shift in your spiritual awareness?

Explanatory Note:

By pinpointing situations where you realized that your ego, often driven by pride and superficial desires, does not define your true self. By listing specific triggers, you can better understand the circumstances that facilitated these transformative experiences, aiding in your ongoing journey of self-discovery and spiritual development.

8.3 Can you think of role models whose wise counsel significantly influenced your thinking and set you on a path of self-reflection, especially during times of dullness or self-indulgence? Reflect on these individuals and describe how they have shaped your personal growth and understanding.

Explanatory Note:

By expressing gratitude, especially during times of stagnation or overindulgence, you can gain a deeper appreciation for the influence these role models have had on your personal growth and development. This reflection can help you understand the significance of their guidance in shaping your journey toward self-improvement.

8.4 Can you identify the pivotal moments in your life that led to profound changes and inspired you to pursue a deeper sense of purpose?

Reflect on these moments and consider the leaps of faith that sparked these significant transformations.

Explanatory Note:

Identifying and reflecting on the turning points in your life allows you to understand the moments that spurred significant personal growth. By recalling the specific leaps of faith you took, you can appreciate the courage and determination that guided you through these transformative experiences, helping you find deeper meaning and purpose in your journey.

8.5 Can you reflect on the ways you've managed delays, failures, and setbacks that have hindered your aspirations?

What strategies have you found effective in navigating these challenging times?

Explanatory Note:

Understanding how you managed delays, failures, and setbacks provides valuable insights into your resilience and determination. Recognizing the coping strategies, you used during these times helps you identify the tools and strengths that supported you. This reflection allows you to apply these lessons to future challenges, ensuring you maintain a positive, forward-moving mindset.

*Reflecting on how you **stayed positive and hopeful** during challenging times is crucial. Consider how seeking inspiration from role models or mentors who had overcome similar obstacles might have provided the encouragement and perspective needed to keep going.*

*Think about the practical steps you took to overcome setbacks, such as **breaking down goals into smaller tasks** to maintain progress and motivation. This approach can* *help achieve incremental successes, even when faced with larger challenges.*

*Consider the importance of self-care and balance in your life. Engaging in activities like **exercise, meditation, or spending time** with loved ones can help maintain resilience and a positive outlook.*

*Lastly, consider how you **adapted** your plans in response to setbacks, viewing failures as opportunities for growth. This mindset shift allows for innovation and finding new solutions, ultimately leading to personal and professional development.*

By reflecting on these aspects, you can gain a deeper understanding of your resilience and the positive coping strategies that have supported you.

Recognize the strengths and tools you've cultivated and consider how to apply these lessons to future challenges.

Chapter 9

Reaching Lanka, Searching for Sita, Ravana and Seeta Encounter-Hanuman Meets Sita... Setting Fire to Lanka

9.1 Journey Over the Ocean

In the Valmiki Ramayana, Hanuman flies across the ocean. After being reminded of his immense capabilities by Jambavan, Hanuman takes a mighty leap from the southern coast of India, propelling himself into the sky with his powerful legs. His journey is marked by several encounters and obstacles.

As Hanuman flies over the ocean, Mainaka, a mountain with the ability to move, rises from the ocean's depths to offer him rest. Mainaka, sent by the ocean god Samudra, represents the offer of respite and support. Hanuman graciously acknowledges the offer but declines, determined to complete his mission without delay.

Next, Hanuman encounters Surasa, a sea goddess and mother of serpents, who tests his resolve. Surasa demands that Hanuman enter her mouth before continuing his journey, symbolizing a trial of will and determination. Hanuman cleverly outwits her by expanding his size, then suddenly shrinking and swiftly entering and exiting her mouth, thereby fulfilling her demand without harm. Surasa blesses him and allows him to continue, recognizing his cleverness and determination.

Simhika, a demoness with the power to grab shadows and drag her prey into the ocean, is the next obstacle. She seizes Hanuman's shadow, pulling him down toward the ocean. Hanuman, realizing the threat, dives into her mouth and tears her apart from the inside, symbolizing the need to confront and overcome hidden dangers and inner fears directly.

Upon reaching the shores of Lanka, Hanuman's journey continues with him taking on a more discreet approach. He shrinks in size to avoid detection and sneaks into the city at night. As he explores Lanka, he is confronted by Lankini, the formidable guardian of the city gates.

Lankini, the guardian of Lanka, challenges Hanuman and tries to stop him from entering the city. Hanuman strikes her with a mighty blow, knocking her down. Realizing his divine mission, Lankini blesses him and allows him to proceed, acknowledging that the fall of Lanka is imminent with Hanuman's arrival.

Delving Deeper....

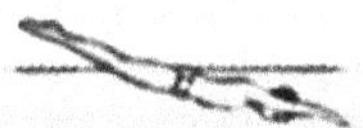

Hanuman's journey over the ocean can be interpreted as the challenges and obstacles a young adult faces while pursuing a significant goal or mission.

The offer of rest by Mainaka represents temptations to take a break or pause, which can be both helpful and distracting. Hanuman's decision to continue his mission symbolizes the importance of staying focused and not succumbing to distractions and delays.

Surasa's challenge symbolizes the trials and tests of will power and cleverness. Overcoming Surasa by outwitting her demonstrates the need for intelligence and resourcefulness in the face of difficulties.

Simhika represents hidden dangers and internal fears that can drag one down. Hanuman's victory over Simhika highlights the importance of confronting and overcoming these fears directly. The shadow represents fears that slow down your progress,

The encounter with Lankini symbolizes the final hurdle before reaching a significant milestone. Hanuman's victory over Lankini and her subsequent blessing represent the recognition of one's purpose and the validation of their mission.

In summary, Hanuman's journey over the ocean and the various encounters he faces highlight the importance of determination, intelligence, courage, and focus on overcoming obstacles. This event emphasizes the need for perseverance and the ability to confront and navigate challenges to achieve one's goals.

9.2 Search for Sita in Lanka and survey of city and Ravana's palace

After entering Lanka, Hanuman explores the city with caution and curiosity. He witnesses the grandeur and opulence of Ravana's kingdom, observing both its splendour and its moral decay. As he surveys the city, he sees its residents indulging in various hedonistic activities, highlighting the contrast between the city's material wealth and its ethical downfall.

Hanuman makes his way to Ravana's palace, an architectural marvel that epitomizes luxury and excess. The palace is adorned with precious gems, intricate carvings, and lavish decorations. Inside, Hanuman sees Ravana surrounded by his many wives and concubines, engaged in decadent feasting and revelry. This scene underscores the hedonistic lifestyle that pervades Ravana's court, characterized by indulgence in sensual pleasures and a blatant disregard for moral values. He even sees the Pushpaka Vimana and it is described in Sundara Kanda (see sec 9.3)

Determined to find Sita, Hanuman continues his search within the palace grounds. He enters various chambers and gardens, encountering numerous rakshasas and witnessing more scenes of debauchery. Despite the temptations and distractions, Hanuman remains focused on his mission.

As Hanuman searches the palaces and still does not find Sita, grave doubts arise in his mind. He begins to fear that he may have failed in his mission. However, Hanuman overcomes these self-doubts by recalling his devotion to Rama and his duty. He regains his resolve and decides to continue his search, driven by his faith and determination.

Eventually, Hanuman arrives at the Ashoka Vatika, a beautiful grove filled with lush greenery, vibrant flowers, and serene ambiance. It is here that Hanuman's perseverance is rewarded. Amidst the tranquillity of the grove, he spots a solitary and sorrowful figure, sitting under a tree. Hanuman realizes that this forlorn woman is none other than Sita, the very person he has been seeking.

Hanuman observes Sita closely and sees her distress and anguish. She is surrounded by rakshasis who guard her and try to intimidate her, but Sita remains steadfast in her devotion to Rama. Despite her dire situation, she exudes a sense of purity and unwavering faith, which deeply moves Hanuman.

Delving Deeper....

Hanuman's survey of Lanka and his eventual discovery of Sita can be seen as a metaphor for a young adult's journey through life, encountering and overcoming moral and ethical challenges while searching for true purpose and meaning.

The city of Lanka, with its grandeur and hedonistic lifestyle, represents the temptations and distractions of material wealth and sensory pleasures that can lead one astray. The city's moral decay contrasts sharply with its physical beauty, highlighting the dangers of losing oneself to excess and indulgence.

Ravana's palace symbolizes the peak of material success and sensual gratification, often accompanied by moral corruption. Hanuman's ability to remain focused amidst the decadence signifies the importance of staying true to one's values and mission despite external temptations.

Hanuman's moments of self-doubt symbolize the internal struggles and uncertainties that arise when one faces difficulties and setbacks. Overcoming these doubts through faith and determination highlights the importance of inner strength and resilience.

The Ashoka Vatika represents a place of inner peace and purity, where true purpose and faith can be found. Hanuman's discovery of Sita in the grove symbolizes the realization of one's higher goals and the importance of maintaining faith and virtue in the face of adversity.

Sita's steadfastness and unwavering devotion to Rama amidst her captivity represent the inner core of faith and integrity that remains untarnished despite external challenges. Hanuman's encounter with Sita underscores the importance of finding and holding onto one's true values and purpose.

In summary, Hanuman's journey through Lanka and his discovery of Sita serves as a powerful metaphor for the challenges and temptations faced in life. It emphasizes the need for perseverance, focus, and moral integrity in the pursuit of true purpose and meaning. It also highlights the significance of overcoming self-doubt and staying true to one's mission.

9.3 Pushpaka Vimana

The description of the Pushpaka Vimana, as narrated in the Sundara Kanda of the Valmiki Ramayana, offers a vivid glimpse into the ancient world's imagination of flight.

Hanuman first encounters this marvel as he scouts Lanka, setting the stage for dramatic revelations.

The Pushpaka Vimana transcends its role as a mere vehicle in the Ramayana, embodying deeper narrative elements and symbolisms. Initially, it serves as the means for Ravana's abduction of Sita, setting the stage for the epic's dramatic unfolding. The Vimana later reveals the war's illusions, including the fabricated deaths of Rama and Lakshman, which deepen Sita's despair while illuminating the profound ramifications of the conflict.

As the story progresses, the Pushpaka Vimana transforms into a symbol of redemption and restoration. It safely transports Rama, Sita, Lakshman, Vanaras and Vibhishana to Ayodhya, marking not only a return to their kingdom but also a moral and spiritual reinstatement of dharma. In the end, Rama's act of returning the Vimana to Kubera, its rightful owner, underscores a commitment to righteousness and the re-establishment of order.

In Sundara Kanda, Hanuman describes the Pushpaka Vimana's mystical capabilities, noting its ability to adjust its size to accommodate its passengers and to travel at the speed of thought. The luxurious interiors, equipped with every conceivable comfort, symbolize the zenith of divine craftsmanship and celestial luxury, illustrating its role as a vessel beyond ordinary understanding.

The Vimana transcends the conventional boundaries of physical mechanics, typical of the fantastical elements found in ancient epics, suggesting its operation on divine or celestial principles.

In "Ramayana Secrets," the Pushpaka Vimana is interpreted as a metaphor for the profound capabilities of the mind and spirit. This interpretation suggests that the Vimana, moving at the speed of thought, is less a physical vehicle and more a conduit for spiritual journeys.

This broader interpretation aligns with the depiction of its passengers—spiritual beings like Rama, Sita, and Lakshman, Vanaras as well as Ravana—whose travels on the vimana symbolize their own spiritual journeys and trials.

Viewing the Pushpaka Vimana as a metaphor for the mind's ability to flower and bloom, as per the driver's intention offers a profound insight into its name.

This idea explains why archaeological efforts fail to uncover such artifacts; the Vimana is not an object to be discovered but a symbol within the narrative to illustrate the expansive capabilities of the mind and spirit and available to anybody and aligned to both Rama and Ravana

9.4 Witnessing the Ravana Sita Interaction

Upon reaching the Ashoka Vatika, Hanuman carefully surveys the grove, a beautiful but heavily guarded garden filled with lush vegetation and fragrant flowers. The tranquillity of the grove stands in stark contrast to the sorrow and despair he sees in Sita, who is sitting under a large Ashoka tree. Hanuman observes Sita's pained demeanour, her frail condition, and the rakshasis' who surround her, taunting and threatening her to submit to Ravana's advances.

Shortly after Hanuman's arrival, Ravana enters the Ashoka Vatika, accompanied by his entourage. Hanuman watches as Ravana approaches Sita, adorned in his regal finery, attempting to impress her with his grandeur and authority. Ravana's intentions are clear—he wants Sita to become his consort and submit to his power. He tries to woo her with promises of wealth, power, and comfort, but Sita remains resolute and unwavering in her devotion to Rama.

Ravana speaks to Sita with a mix of coercion and persuasion, trying to break her spirit. He reminds her of his might and the futility of waiting for Rama, whom he belittles as powerless against him. Despite Ravana's threats and temptations, Sita responds with calm defiance. She firmly declares her unwavering loyalty to Rama, rejecting Ravana's advances and steadfastly maintaining her chastity and devotion. Her dignity and strength in the face of Ravana's advances highlight her unwavering faith.

Hanuman, hidden among the foliage, feels a surge of admiration for Sita's courage and strength. He realizes that her unwavering faith in Rama are the very qualities that will ultimately lead to her rescue and the downfall of Ravana. Hanuman's faith and devotion in Rama and the righteousness of their mission is further strengthened by witnessing Sita's unyielding spirit.

Hanuman's observations of Sita and Ravana's exchanges in the Ashoka Vatika represent a pivotal moment in the Sundara Kanda, showcasing the profound connection between devotion (Hanuman) and faith (Sita). Hanuman's presence underscores how devotion reinforces and supports faith, while Sita's unwavering resolve in the face of Ravana's pressures highlights the strength of inner conviction. This encounter emphasizes the importance of upholding one's principles and faith amidst overwhelming temptation and adversity, demonstrating how devotion and faith can triumph over ego and material allurements.

Delving Deeper....

In a broader allegorical sense, this part of the Ramayana teaches that true faith and devotion can withstand any challenge, and that the union of these qualities is essential for overcoming adversity and achieving one's higher purpose. It also emphasizes that the ego and its temptations, represented by Ravana, can be resisted through unwavering devotion and faith, ultimately leading to spiritual triumph and liberation.

This scene marks a crucial moment in the epic, showcasing the indomitable spirit of faith and the pivotal role of devotion in the quest for righteousness and liberation.

9.5 Hanuman Sita Interactions

After observing the exchanges between Sita and Ravana, Hanuman decides it is time to reveal himself. He carefully approaches Sita, who is in a state of despair, and begins to softly chant the praises of Rama from his hiding place. Sita, initially startled, looks around to find the source of the chanting. Hanuman then gently drops from the tree and introduces himself as a messenger of Rama.

Hanuman respectfully bows to Sita and presents himself as a devoted servant of Rama. He explains how he came to find her, relaying the events that led him to Lanka and the perilous journey he undertook. Hanuman shows Sita the ring given to him by Rama as proof of his authenticity. This sight brings a glimmer of hope to Sita, who had been tormented by Ravana's advances and her prolonged separation from Rama.

Hanuman's words are filled with reverence and compassion, offering Sita the solace she desperately needs. He reassures her that Rama is tirelessly working to rescue her and that their reunion is imminent. This conversation symbolizes the profound connection between faith (Sita) and devotion (Hanuman). Hanuman's unwavering devotion to Rama mirrors Sita's steadfast faith, illustrating how these two qualities support and reinforce each other on the path to spiritual evolution.

This meeting between Hanuman and Sita is one of the most poignant and spiritually significant episodes in the Ramayana. It showcases the power of devotion to bring comfort and hope to faith. The Sundara Kanda, therefore, holds a special place in the hearts of devotees, symbolizing the eternal bond between faith and devotion that sustains and guides the soul on its spiritual journey.

Hanuman's meeting with Sita in the Ashoka Vatika is a defining moment in the Sundara Kanda. His assurances and Sita's expressions of gratitude highlight the profound connection between faith and devotion. This episode underscores how devotion provides solace and strength to faith, illustrating the core principles of spiritual evolution. The Sundara Kanda's popularity stems from its depiction of this powerful and uplifting interaction, showcasing the eternal bond between faith and devotion as the foundation of the spiritual path.

Delving Deeper....

The dialogue between Hanuman and Sita highlights several key metaphoric elements:

- Devotion's Assurance: Hanuman's arrival and his comforting words symbolize how devotion brings reassurance and hope to faith during times of distress.

- Faith's Gratitude: Sita's response to Hanuman's assurances reflects how faith, when supported by devotion, can find solace and strength even in the direst circumstances.

- Spiritual Bedrock: This interaction emphasizes that faith and devotion are the twin pillars of spiritual growth. Just as Hanuman's devotion drives him to leap across the ocean, Sita's unwavering faith sustains her through her captivity.

Expression of Gratitude

Sita, deeply moved by Hanuman's dedication and the message he brings, expresses her heartfelt gratitude. She acknowledges the immense risk Hanuman took to find her and the comfort his presence provides. Sita gives Hanuman a jewel from her hair to take back to Rama as a token of her love and a sign of her continued faithfulness. In some other retellings it is said that Sita offers a garland made of betel leaf and flowers to Hanuman.

Hanuman's encounter with Sita is a moment of deep devotion and reassurance. After giving her Rama's ring, Hanuman spoke with reverence, assuring Sita of Rama's unwavering love and devotion. He described his bond with Rama as one of unbreakable loyalty and love, emphasizing how deeply Rama was suffering from their separation and how tirelessly he was working to rescue her.

Hanuman humbly acknowledged that the extraordinary feats he had accomplished—crossing the ocean, infiltrating Lanka, and finding her—were all due to Rama's divine power. He attributed his strength and success entirely to Rama's grace, explaining that his abilities reflected Rama's power working through him.

Through his words, Hanuman offered Sita profound reassurance, reminding her that she was never alone, and that Rama's love would soon bring them back together. His interaction with Sita was a testament to the depth of his devotion and the power of Rama's love, offering Sita hope and comfort in her darkest hour.

9.6 Hanumans boisterous activities, his captivity and direct encounter with Ravana and setting fire to Lanka

After meeting and comforting Sita, Hanuman decides to assess the strength of Lanka's defences and cause some disruption. He begins by destroying the Ashoka Vatika, the garden where Sita is held captive. Hanuman uproots trees, tramples plants, and creates havoc, which alarms the Rakshasas guarding the area.

As the chaos escalates, Hanuman encounters several Rakshasas. He engages in fierce battles, killing many, including Akshayakumar, one of Ravana's sons. Despite his formidable strength, Hanuman is eventually captured by Indrajit, Ravana's son, using the powerful Brahmastra.

Bound by the Brahmastra, Hanuman is brought before Ravana. Despite being restrained, Hanuman remains fearless and confronts Ravana with confidence. He boldly declares his mission and warns Ravana of Rama's impending attack if Sita is not released. Hanuman's words and demeanour infuriate Ravana.

During this interaction, Hanuman also speaks as an emissary for Rama, delivering his message with unwavering resolve. In the court, he meets Vibhishana, Ravana's righteous brother, who supports Hanuman's mission and words.

Ravana, enraged by Hanuman's defiance, orders his men to set Hanuman's tail on fire as punishment. However, Hanuman uses this to his advantage. Once his tail is ablaze, he breaks free from his bonds and leaps from building to building, setting Lanka aflame. The city is engulfed in chaos and fear as the fire spreads rapidly, causing significant destruction. The citizens of Lanka are shaken to their core by the unexpected devastation.

In Valmiki Ramayana it is stated that when Sita hears that Hanuman's tail has been set on fire by Ravana's forces, she is deeply distressed. Recognizing Hanuman's courage and devotion and feeling a profound sense of responsibility for his safety, Sita prays earnestly to Agni, the god of fire. With a heart full of purity and devotion, she asks Agni to protect Hanuman and keep his tail cool despite the flames. Touched by Sita's unwavering faith and the sincerity of her prayers, Agni ensures that the fire does not harm Hanuman. As a result, though surrounded by flames, Hanuman remains unharmed, and his tail stays cool. This powerful episode highlights not only the protective power of Sita's prayers but also the deep, spiritual bond between her and Hanuman, illustrating how devotion and righteousness can triumph even in the face of great adversity.

After causing extensive damage, Hanuman extinguishes his burning tail in the sea and returns to Rama with the news of Sita's whereabouts and his observations in Lanka. The burning of Hanuman's tail, intended by Ravana to unsettle him, backfires spectacularly, instead causing fear and confusion among the citizens of Lanka.

Delving Deeper....

.... Lanka's destruction ... Destiny or Free will....

Hanuman's destruction of Lanka symbolizes a young adult's awakening to the emptiness of hedonistic pursuits. The lush allure of Lanka's gardens and grand palaces epitomizes the temptations of sensory pleasures and material indulgence.

Hanuman's act of uprooting these symbols reflects a crucial moment of realization: seeing through the superficial allure and recognizing the transient nature of such pursuits.

His actions underscore the importance of discarding unrestrained self-interest to embrace a higher, more meaningful purpose, which is vital for personal growth and realizing one's true potential. Hanuman's fearlessness in confronting Ravana, undeterred by threats or power, illustrates the need for steadfastness in one's convictions and the pursuit of integrity, regardless of the distractions and challenges that abound.

The transformative fire Hanuman sets in Lanka is a metaphor for internal change—burning away old, destructive patterns to foster new growth and understanding. This intense process, though potentially painful, paves the way for a fulfilling and purpose-driven life.

For young adults, the need to remain steadfast arises particularly when faced with numerous options that might pull their focus in various directions. In today's fast-paced world, where changing jobs, relocating, or shifting careers is common, the challenge lies in maintaining a consistent path despite these external changes. Feeling the need to remain steadfast often comes from a deeper understanding of one's core values and long-term goals. This understanding helps young adults resist fleeting temptations and stay committed to their chosen path, even when easier or more enticing alternatives are available.

The necessity for steadfastness can also arise from grappling with extreme uncertainty, such as joblessness, pervasive low self-esteem, or the troubling sensation of not having discovered one's life purpose. In these challenging times, young adults may feel as though they are lost in the wilderness of life, much like wandering in an unfamiliar, daunting forest without a clear path forward.

This sense of being adrift can profoundly test one's resolve, making the cultivation of steadfastness not just beneficial but essential for navigating through the fog of life's uncertainties. Steadfastness provides a psychological anchor, offering stability and a sense of direction when external circumstances fluctuate wildly or when personal aspirations seem distant. Building resilience through steadfast commitment to personal values and goals can transform these overwhelming challenges into opportunities for growth and self-realization.

Incorporating routines that reinforce self-worth and purpose, seeking supportive communities, and embracing continuous learning are ways to foster this quality. This internal compass becomes crucial in maintaining focus and motivation amidst life's inevitable upheavals, guiding young adults toward a fulfilling path, much like Hanuman's unwavering dedication led to profound achievements despite the daunting obstacles he faced.

For those lacking these qualities, developing them involves cultivating awareness, seeking mentorship, and engaging in practices that promote discipline and reflection. Establishing a clear set of values and regularly evaluating one's actions against these ideals can help maintain focus and integrity, even when faced with numerous options and potential distractions.

Hanuman's journey through Lanka is not just a tale of physical bravery but also a metaphorical map for young adults navigating the complexities of growth and self-discovery. It highlights the importance of sacrificing fleeting pleasures for lasting fulfilment and integrity, echoing the deeper themes of the Ramayana in personal and spiritual evolution.

9.7 Return to the shore …Vanara army rejoices…. At Kishkindha with Rama …next move

After setting Lanka on fire, Hanuman's heart is filled with concern for Sita's safety. He returns to Ashoka Vatika to ensure that no harm has come to her due to the fire. To his relief, he finds Sita safe and unharmed. He reassures her of Rama's imminent arrival and then prepares for his journey back.

Hanuman returns over the ocean, retracing his path from Lanka to the shore where the Vanaras await him. His return is marked by the same incredible speed and agility that characterized his initial journey.

Upon reaching the shore, Hanuman is greeted with joy and anticipation by the Vanaras. He narrates his meeting with Sita, providing vivid descriptions of her condition and her unwavering faith in Rama. This news brings immense relief and joy to the Vanaras, particularly the southern search party led by Angada. Hanuman bows down in the direction of Lanka where Sita is held captive and all the Vanaras present understand that there is a great mission ahead and its urgency.

Angada suggests that they should go immediately to Lanka and rescue Sita. However, after some discussions they decide to return to Kishkindha to inform Rama and Sugreeva of the successful discovery of Sita. Since this was the initial instruction, this plan is supported by all, especially Jambavan, who emphasizes the importance of delivering the good news without delay and await the plans that will be decided so that the entire Vanara army from all directions can be mobilized. The two months period that Sita indicated should be sufficient to plan well.

Before heading back to Kishkindha, the Vanaras, including Hanuman, indulge in wanton rejoicing in the Madhuban, a luscious garden owned by Sugreeva's uncle. They celebrate their success with great exuberance, feasting and making merry, which serves to uplift their spirits further.

Finally, the Vanaras reach Kishkindha and present themselves before Rama. Hanuman recounts his journey, his meeting with Sita, and the details of Lanka, carefully avoiding his heroic exploits. He focuses on the crucial information: Sita is safe, but there is an urgent need to rescue her. His description of Sita's condition and his assurances of her unwavering devotion fill Rama with hope and determination.

He hands over the crest jewel and narrates a secret story that Sita narrated to Hanuman about the crow in Chitrakoot. Hearing all this Rama, Lakshman and Sugreeva were spurred to plan their return to Lanka with the full Vanara Army.

Delving Deeper....

Hanuman's return to check on Sita's safety emphasizes the responsibility and care that come with discovering a higher purpose. For young adults, this highlights the importance of ensuring their actions do not cause unintended harm, reflecting the maturity needed in pursuing their goals.

The Vanaras' celebration in Madhuban symbolizes the joy of achieving milestones on the path to personal growth. It underscores the need to rejoice and recharge after success, while also preparing for future challenges.

Hanuman's humility in recounting his exploits to Rama underscores the importance of staying focused on the larger mission rather than seeking personal glory. For young adults, this humility is crucial in maintaining the integrity of their purpose, ensuring success is met with equanimity.

Hanuman's urgent message to Rama illustrates the need for timely action and determination in achieving goals. For young adults, it serves as a reminder to stay committed, proactive, and focused, transforming newfound purpose into sustained effort and meaningful impact.

The conclusion of the Sundara Kanda brings together moments of responsibility, celebration, humility, and urgency. For young adults, these moments emphasize the importance of caring for others, celebrating achievements, practicing humility, and acting with resolve. It also underscores the value of self-reflection—assessing one's journey, learning from experiences, and realigning with goals. These qualities are essential for turning initial success into a fulfilling and purposeful life journey toward realizing one's higher purpose.

Five Self-Reflection questions

9.1 Reflect on vision and mission that Rama and Vanaras shared

Explanatory Note:

Understanding the vision and mission shared by Rama and the Vanaras provides valuable insights into the power of collective purpose and dedication. Reflecting on these shared goals can help you identify the principles and values that drive successful collaboration and unity. This reflection allows you to draw parallels to your own experiences, recognize the importance of a shared vision, and apply these lessons to foster teamwork and achieve common objectives in your personal and professional life.

9.2 Can you identify the key points in your life when you truly understood your calling?

List how you recalibrated your mission and gained clarity on the wrong priorities you were previously pursuing?

Explanatory Note:

Recognizing the moments when you discovered your true calling helps to highlight your journey of self-awareness and personal growth. Reflecting on how you adjusted your mission and corrected your course can provide insight into your values and decision-making processes, allowing you to align more closely with your authentic self and long-term goals.

9.3 Can you identify how you implemented changes and reoriented your priorities? What activities did you refocus on, and which ones did you let go?

Explanation

Evaluating how you adjusted your priorities and the steps you took to implement these changes reveals your adaptability and commitment to personal growth. By reflecting on the activities, you chose to focus on and those you decided to abandon, you can gain a deeper understanding of how you align your actions with your newly clarified goals and values, ensuring that your efforts contribute meaningfully to your overall vision and well-being.

9.4 Can you identify how you went about implementing changes and reorienting your priorities? What specific activities did you choose to refocus on, and which ones did you decide to let go?

Explanation

By detailing the activities, you chose to emphasize and those you chose to release, you can better understand your decision-making process and how effectively you aligned your daily efforts with your revised goals. This reflection helps clarify how well you've integrated your new priorities into your life and can guide future adjustments for sustained growth and fulfilment.

9.5 Reflect on how you celebrated the changes you made and rejoiced in your newfound clarity. How did this process enhance your inner joy, especially after recognizing the futility of your previous pursuits?

Explanation

Celebrating these milestones in the company of wise and supportive individuals can enrich the experience, providing not only a sense of community but also a profound reinforcement of your new path. This shared joy not only affirms your choices but also embeds a deeper, more meaningful sense of happiness and purpose in your life.

This reflection helps you appreciate the transformation process and understand how celebrating milestones contributes to a deeper, more enduring sense of happiness and purpose.

Chapter 10

Mobilizing for Conquest of Lanka... Ravana Also Prepares...

10.1 A huge Vanara army is readied...Rama leads ...march to Southern shore

Upon returning to Rama, Hanuman shares detailed observations about the fortifications of Lanka, emphasizing the island's formidable defences. He conveys Sita's concerns about how the Vanara army could possibly cross the ocean to reach Lanka. This information underscores the challenge ahead and the need for strategic planning and resolve.

Moved by Hanuman's dedication, courage, and the invaluable information he has brought, Rama expresses his deep gratitude. Recognizing Hanuman's crucial role in the quest, Rama embraces him warmly. This act of gratitude and affection strengthens the bond between Rama and Hanuman, affirming the clarity and determination of their mission. This is a crowning moment for Hanuman.

Rama, determined to rescue Sita and undeterred by the obstacles, decides to mobilize a large Vanara army.

Understanding the strength of the well-equipped Lankan forces, as observed by Hanuman, Rama prepares for an arduous campaign.

The Vanaras, led by their capable leaders, begin to gather and organize at the shores of the ocean. There is a clear sense of urgency and purpose as they evaluate various means to cross the vast expanse of water. The preparation involves understanding the logistics, resources, and potential strategies for overcoming the natural barrier.

Lakshman's observations of positive omens and favourable astrological alignments play a crucial role in boosting the morale of Rama's group. These signs—such as the blooming of flowers, auspicious animals, and planetary alignments—are seen as divine approval, instilling hope and confidence in their mission. Conversely, the Rakshasas face negative portents, like the screeching of owls and howling of jackals, signalling their impending doom and weakening their resolve.

These omens and astrological signs reflect the ancient belief that the universe is interconnected and that human actions are influenced by divine will. For Rama's group, the positive omens provide reassurance and strength, while the negative signs for the Rakshasas foreshadow their inevitable defeat. The Ramayana uses these elements to emphasize the importance of aligning with dharma and the cosmic order, suggesting that those who act righteously are supported by the universe, while those who stray face destruction.

To ensure a smooth journey to the southern shore from Kishkindha, Rama had earlier dispatched a forward army group. Their task was to clear the path and minimize damage or inconvenience, demonstrating Rama's strategic foresight and concern for the wellbeing of his troops.

Delving Deeper....

The detailed observations and reports shared by Hanuman represent the need for thorough understanding and strategic planning in any significant undertaking. For a young adult, it signifies the importance of gathering information and planning meticulously when faced with a major challenge.

The collective effort of the Vanaras symbolizes the power of teamwork and collaboration. It highlights the importance of mobilizing resources and working together towards a common goal, a crucial lesson for young adults in their personal and professional lives.

Lakshman's observation of positive omens signifies the importance of recognizing and drawing strength from favourable signs and opportunities. It highlights the role of optimism and confidence in pursuing one's goals as also timings.

This phase of Yuddha Kanda encapsulates key lessons in strategic planning, collaboration, patience, decisive action, and optimism, which are vital for young adults navigating their own life's journeys.

10.2 Ravana prepares… the leadership style… the followers… the ethical orientation…… Vibhishan the lone voice of restraint…

After Hanuman's daring reconnaissance mission, which resulted in significant damage to Lanka and instilled fear among its citizens, Ravana was left shaken. Despite the clear signs of an impending attack, Ravana and his generals were largely unaware of the true strength and nature of the Vanara army since Ravana always dismissed Rama.

Ravana convened a council with his generals to discuss their strategy. The generals, displaying overconfidence, either boasted about their strength or suggested unethical means to subdue Sita. Among these voices, Ravana's own leadership style emerged—rooted in his assumed invincibility and past successes. He boasted about his previous victories and also informed about the curse he had acquired due to past transgressions the reason why he cannot treat Sita as he wishes.

Vibhishana, Ravana's younger brother, stood out as a voice of reason. He advised restraint and urged Ravana to return Sita to avoid further calamity. However, Ravana and his court dismissed Vibhishana's prudent counsel, preferring to rely on their might and fortifications. This dismissal highlighted the flawed nature of Ravana's leadership—driven by ego and a refusal to heed to wise advice.

Despite the overconfidence displayed by his generals, Ravana recognized the need for preparation. He began fortifying the city and readying his forces, though the preparations were marked by an underlying arrogance. The true strength and capabilities of the Vanara army remained largely unknown to him, further contributing to his downfall.

The turning point in the council came when Ravana insulted Vibhishana, leading to a significant rift. Vibhishana, unable to support Ravana's obstinate and reckless decisions, defected to Rama's side. This defection was pivotal, as Vibhishana provided Rama with valuable intelligence about Lanka's defences and Ravana's strategies.

Ravana's forces, bolstered by their leader's confidence and their own hubris, believed themselves to be invincible. They underestimated the Vanara army and Rama's leadership, setting the stage for their eventual defeat. The combination of fortifications, weaponry, and sheer numbers seemed formidable, but the lack of humility and disregard for ethical considerations undermined their efforts.

Delving Deeper....

Ravana was known far and wide for his unparalleled strength and victories. Yet, it was his overconfidence, born from these very successes, that ultimately led to his downfall. For young adults, Ravana's story serves as a powerful reminder that arrogance can be blinding. No matter how successful one has been in the past, humility is crucial. The willingness to learn, adapt, and acknowledge one's limitations is what truly defines enduring leadership.

Throughout the conflict, Vibhishana, Ravana's own brother, repeatedly offered wise and reasoned counsel, urging Ravana to reconsider his actions. But Ravana, blinded by his pride, dismissed these warnings. This act of disregarding valuable advice teaches an important lesson: even when advice challenges our beliefs or desires, it is essential to listen. Heeding wise counsel, especially from those who have our best interests at heart, can be the difference between triumph and disaster.

In contrast to Vibhishana's moral integrity, many of Ravana's generals encouraged unethical tactics to win the war. This stark difference emphasizes the importance of ethical decision-making in leadership. True leadership is not just about achieving goals but doing so in a way that upholds integrity and moral values. Young adults can learn that the path to success is not worth pursuing if it means compromising on what is right.

Ravana's preparation for battle, though grand in terms of fortifications and weaponry, lacked crucial elements of intelligence and strategic foresight. He underestimated the strength and determination of the Vanara army, led by Rama. This oversight teaches a critical lesson: it's not just about having the resources but also about understanding the adversary, anticipating challenges, and being strategically prepared.

The discord within Ravana's ranks, culminating in Vibhishana's defection, highlights the importance of team cohesion and respect. A leader must value diverse perspectives and foster an environment where all voices are heard and respected. When team dynamics are fractured, success becomes elusive. This lesson is particularly relevant for young adults, emphasizing the need for unity, collaboration, and mutual respect in any group endeavor.

In the end, Ravana's leadership, marked by pride, ethical lapses, and ignored counsel, serves as a cautionary tale. It reminds young adults of the importance of humility, ethical conduct, and the value of listening to wise advice. These are the true hallmarks of leadership that withstand the test of time.

10.3 Vibhishana joins Rama…Vanara army builds the Setu …

Initially, Rama's allies were sceptical of Vibhishana's intentions. However, Hanuman supported Vibhishana by recalling Sita's mention of Vibhishana's desire to see her freed. Hanuman vouched for Vibhishana's sincerity, and his counsel played a crucial role in swaying Rama. Ultimately, Rama, with his inherent compassion and wisdom, chose to accept Vibhishana, believing in his genuine repentance and loyalty. Rama's decision underscored his commitment to dharma and his willingness to give a chance to those seeking redemption.

To undermine the unity between Rama and Sugreeva's forces, Ravana sent an emissary to Sugreeva, Shuka, trying to break their alliance through devious methods with friendship overtures. However, Sugreeva, with his unwavering loyalty to Rama, strongly rebutted the emissary's attempts, reinforcing the bond between the Vanaras and Rama. This incident highlighted Ravana's reliance on deceit and the steadfast unity and determination of Rama's allies.

Once accepted, Vibhishana became a valuable advisor to Rama. He suggested that Rama seek the support of the ocean god to facilitate the crossing to Lanka. Rama, heeding this advice, began a penance on the shores, seeking the ocean god's help. However, when the ocean god did not initially respond, Rama grew impatient and prepared to use his divine weapons to dry up the ocean.

Impressed by Rama's determination, the ocean god eventually appeared and promised to aid him. He suggested building a bridge (Setu) and assured Rama that he would keep the waters calm and low to facilitate the construction. This divine intervention reinforced the righteousness of Rama's cause and his unwavering resolve.

Under the leadership of Nala, a Vanara known for his engineering skills, the Vanara army began constructing the Setu (bridge) to Lanka. Contrary to popular belief, the Valmiki Ramayana does not describe the bridge as a floating structure but rather as a solid bund formed by dumping rocks and tree trunks into the sea, building upon the sea bottom. The Vanaras worked tirelessly, placing large boulders, stones, and logs to create a sturdy pathway across the ocean. This monumental effort highlighted their unity, determination, and unwavering dedication to Rama's mission.

The Setu symbolized the overcoming of seemingly insurmountable obstacles through faith, perseverance, and collective effort. It bridged the gap between the mainland and Lanka, representing the connection between the subtle realm and the kingdom of sensory pursuits, which Rama aimed to conquer.

Delving Deeper....

Vibhishana, brother of the demon king Ravana, made a pivotal decision that would change the course of the war. Realizing the darkness that had consumed his family, Vibhishana sought redemption by leaving his brother's side to join Rama. This act of defection was not just a strategic move but a profound lesson in the importance of recognizing one's mistakes and seeking a path of righteousness. It also highlighted Rama's compassion, as he welcomed Vibhishana with open arms, demonstrating the value of forgiveness and the power of giving others a second chance.

As the battle plans unfolded, it was Vibhishana's wise counsel that guided Rama to seek the help of the ocean god, Samudra, in constructing the bridge to Lanka. His advice underscores the importance of listening to those with experience and wisdom, a lesson that young adults can carry with them as they navigate the complexities of life. It teaches the value of humility in recognizing that others' guidance can be instrumental in overcoming challenges.

Rama's journey was not without its struggles. His initial impatience with the ocean god, followed by his determination to seek divine intervention, serves as a powerful reminder of the balance between action and patience. For young adults, this episode is a testament to the idea that while persistence is crucial, so is the understanding that some things require time and divine timing to manifest.

The construction of the Nal Setu, the bridge to Lanka, was a monumental task, achieved only through the collective effort of Rama's Vanara army. This momentous feat symbolizes the strength found in unity and teamwork. It shows that even the most daunting challenges can be overcome when individuals work together toward a common goal. For young adults, it's a lesson in the power of collaboration and the incredible things that can be achieved through collective effort.

Finally, the Nal Setu itself, bridging the gap between the world of sensory pursuits and the path of righteousness, stands as a metaphor for the journey toward self-realization. Lanka, the land of hedonistic desires, represents the distractions that can lead one astray. The bridge signifies the determination to overcome these distractions and strive for a higher purpose. This journey, reflected in the construction of the Setu, is one of the most important lessons for those at the crossroads of life, reminding them to seek a path of virtue and self-discipline.

Through Vibhishana's defection and the construction of the Nal Setu, young adults are offered valuable insights into leadership, redemption, collective effort, and the pursuit of righteousness—essential lessons as they navigate their own life journeys.

10.4 Nal Setu - Bridging the Mind to Transcend the Ego

Nal Setu, or the bridge to Lanka, serves as a profound symbol of the journey toward spiritual enlightenment. Constructed by the Vanaras under the divine guidance of Lord Rama, this bridge represents the vital connection between the forces of the mind and the endeavour to breach the fortifications of the senses and ego, symbolized by Ravana and his stronghold of Lanka.

The Vanaras, seen as personification of the untamed mind, signify our thoughts, emotions, and impulses. By organizing these forces under a divine mission, the construction of Nal Setu illustrates the harnessing of the mind's chaotic energies towards a higher purpose. The bridge itself becomes a metaphor for the essential path we must build within ourselves to overcome the ensnaring grip of our senses and ego.

Valmiki's vivid descriptions of the bridge's construction using rocks and uprooted tree trunks carry deep symbolic meaning. The rocks represent firm and often rigid belief systems that need to be shattered or transformed. Stoning these beliefs symbolizes the active effort required to break down hard, ingrained patterns of thought that impede spiritual progress. The uprooted tree trunks, on the other hand, signify the need to transcend and uproot the deep-seated attachments and desires that bind us to the material world. By pulling these trees from their roots, the Vanaras illustrate the necessity of confronting and removing the very foundations of our sensory and ego-driven existence.

Without this symbolic bridge, one remains ensconced by the senses and ego, unable to reach the divine potential within. Nal Setu teaches us that to achieve true spiritual liberation, we must construct our own bridges of self-discipline, mindfulness, and devotion. This bridge helps us cross the turbulent ocean of material existence and achieve the serene shores of higher consciousness. The divine support for this quest is illustrated by the blessing of the lord of the sea, who appears and creates a conducive environment for the bridge's construction.

In essence, Nal Setu is not just a physical structure in the epic but a spiritual metaphor for the inner journey we must undertake. It reminds us that through determined effort and divine guidance, we can connect the forces of our mind, overcome the fortifications of the senses and ego, and ultimately achieve spiritual freedom.

10.5 At Lanka... preparations. deceptions, spy work

After successfully constructing the Setu and crossing the ocean, Rama and his allies set up camp outside the gates of Lanka. They positioned themselves strategically to prepare for the impending battle against Ravana's forces. The camp was bustling with activity as the Vanara army, under the leadership of Rama, Sugreeva, Hanuman, and other key leaders, made final preparations for the confrontation.

Shuka, a spy sent by Ravana, advised the demon king of the impending battle. Despite Shuka's warnings about the formidable strength of Rama and his allies, Ravana arrogantly dismissed the concerns. He boasted of his power and the invincibility of his forces, showing his overconfidence and disdain for his adversaries.

Determined to gather intelligence on Rama's army, Ravana dispatched Shuka and another spy, Sarana, to infiltrate the enemy camp and report on how they crossed of the ocean, the arms they possessed, and their leaders. However, both spies were caught by Rama's forces. Displaying his characteristic magnanimity, Rama chose to let them go. Shuka and Sarana returned to Ravana, reporting not only the strength of Rama's army but also Rama's cordial and honourable treatment, reinforcing the stark contrast between the two leaders.

In a bid to demoralize Sita and Rama's forces, Ravana employed another devious tactic. He ordered the creation of an illusion of Rama's severed head and presented it to Sita. This cruel trick was intended to break Sita's spirit and convince her of Rama's death. However, Sita's anguish was short-lived, thanks to the intervention of Sarama, a rakshasi sympathetic to her plight, who is also Vibhishana's wife.

Sarama, who had been secretly aiding Sita, revealed the truth about Ravana's deception. She reassured Sita that Rama was alive and had already crossed into Lanka with his army. This revelation restored Sita's hope and resolve. Sita then requested Sarama to spy on Ravana and gather information about his plans, further bolstering her faith in Rama's eventual victory.

With the knowledge of Ravana's impending moves, Rama and his allies finalized their battle strategies. The Vanara army, driven by their leaders' resolve and the just mission they were fighting for, prepared for the confrontation. Ravana, despite his arrogance, also mobilized his formidable forces, readying them for the clash.

Delving Deeper....

For a young adult, these events symbolize the importance of perseverance, integrity, and hope in the face of deceit and adversity. The journey and the preparations for the battle illustrate the necessity of gathering reliable information, building alliances, and maintaining morale, even when facing a seemingly formidable opponent. The stark contrast between Rama's honour and Ravana's deceit serves as a reminder of the values of righteousness and the ultimate triumph of divine over profane.

10.6 The preparation for confrontation

Ravana assigns his generals to guard the gates of Lanka: Prahasta at the eastern gate, Mahaparshva and Mahodara at the southern gate, Indrajit at the western gate, and Ravana himself at the northern gate. Virupaksha is stationed at the centre of the fort.

Hearing Vibhishana's report, Rama assigns Nila to attack the eastern gate, Angad the southern gate, Hanuman the western gate, and Rama and Lakshman the northern gate. Sugreeva, Jambavan, and Vibhishana are positioned at the centre. Rama instructs the Vanaras to remain in their natural forms for easy identification.

Rama, Lakshman, Sugreeva, and Vibhishana ascend Mount Suvela to observe Lanka's beauty and splendour. They were astonished by its magnificence. The Vanaras explore the groves around Lanka, marvelling at the city's grandeur atop Trikuta Mountain.

In a fit of anger, Sugreeva seeing Ravana, attacks him inside Lanka. After a fierce wrestling match, Ravana tries to use his magical powers, prompting Sugreeva to retreat to Rama's side. Rama advises Sugreeva against such reckless actions that do not befit a king.

Rama observes ominous signs of impending destruction as he descends Mount Suvela with the Vanara army. They march to Lanka and besiege the city from all sides, preparing for the battle ahead.

Rama sends Angad to deliver a stern message to Ravana, warning him of the consequences of not returning Sita. Enraged, Ravana orders Angada's capture, but Angada defeats the demons, causes destruction in the palace, and returns to Rama.

Thus, all efforts to avoid the war comes to a stop.

10.7 Eight days of war – the happenings

Day 1

On the first day of the war, the Vanaras breached Lanka's defences, with Hanuman killing Jambumali, Sugreeva defeating Prahasta, and Nila defeating Nikumbha. Lakshman overcame Virupaksha, thus causing four Rakshasa leaders and their forces to retreat. Angad forced Indrajit to fall back, but Indrajit returned invisibly, paralyzing Rama and Lakshman with poison arrows. Mistaking them for dead, Indrajit announced victory, and Ravana showed Sita the battlefield appearing in the Pushpaka Vimana, causing her despair. Despite this, Trijata who was along with Sita and a supporter pointed out that the Vanaras were undeterred, giving hope to Sita. Rama regained consciousness.

Sushena, the physician, identified the medicines need. Garuda then appeared, removing the poison and reviving both brothers and all the Vanaras. By the end of the day, Rama and Lakshman were back on their feet, ready to continue the battle.

Day 2

On the second day of the war, the rejuvenated Vanaras, led by Rama and Lakshman, launched a fierce attack. Sensing trouble, Ravana sent the Rakshasa general Dhumraksha through the western gate, but Hanuman countered and killed him, causing the Rakshasas to retreat. Ravana then dispatched Vajradanstra through the southern gate, where Angad led a deadly fight, ultimately beheading Vajradanstra and causing yet another rakshasha retreat. Finally, Ravana sent Akampana, also through the western gate again. Despite being wounded from Akampana's arrows, Hanuman killed Akampana with a tree trunk, leading to yet another Rakshasa retreat. Hanuman, demonstrating true leadership, thanked the Vanaras and together they roared triumphantly, creating chills in Lanka

Day 3

On the third day of the war, Ravana, after losing four generals, appointed Prahasta to lead the attack from the eastern gate. Nila, the Vanara leader, fiercely battled Prahasta, sustaining severe injuries but ultimately damaging Prahasta's chariot and defeating him with a stone, causing the Rakshasas to retreat. Realizing he had underestimated the Vanaras, Ravana took command himself, emerging from the northern gate in a grand chariot. Rama, now seeing

Ravana for the first time, became furious. Sugreeva initially engaged Ravana but was struck unconscious. As Ravana's arrows incapacitated several Vanara leaders, Hanuman and Nila confronted him too. The battle intensified with Lakshman and Ravana exchanging arrows, resulting in Lakshman being injured and knocked unconscious by a spear from Ravana. Hanuman swiftly rescued Lakshman, and Rama joined the fight against Ravana. Rama's arrows shook Ravana and removed even his crown, prompting Ravana to retreat hastily. Rama and Lakshman then attended to the wounded Vanaras, aware that the battle was far from over.

Day 4

On the fourth day of battle, with Ravana's top generals defeated and having had to retreat himself, Ravana faced a rare moment of self-reflection. In a desperate bid, he awakened the giant Kumbhakarna using a thousand elephants. After a massive meal, Kumbhakarna visited Ravana, who urged him to join the battle. Initially reluctant, Kumbhakarna eventually agreed. Upon entering the fray with his mighty mace, he wreaked havoc, killing many Vanaras and injuring Hanuman. He even captured Sugreeva but was unable to hold him for long. Rama, using the Rudrastra and Vayavastra, managed to cut off Kumbhakarna's arms and legs, eventually decapitating him. Ravana, stunned by the loss of such a formidable warrior, fainted and, for the first time, acknowledged Vibhishana's warnings as true.

Day 5

On the fifth day of battle, following Kumbhakarna's death, Ravana sent his son Atikaya to lead the Rakshasa forces. Atikaya faced Lakshman. who used the Agneastra, but Lakshman ultimately sliced off Atikaya's head. Ravana, now sorrowful and enraged, turned to Indrajit, who entered the battle using his Mayavi powers of illusion. Indrajit, armed with the Brahmastra, incapacitated Sugreeva, Angad, and Nala, and blinded most of the Vanaras. Using his illusionary weapons, Indrajit rendered both Rama and Lakshman unconscious. Vibhishana and Hanuman remained unaffected, and an injured Jambavan instructed Hanuman to fetch four crucial herbs from the Himalayas: Sanjeevani, Vishalyakarani, Sandhanakarani and Savarnyakarani from the Gandamadana mountain. Hanuman grew to an enormous size, leaped to the mountain, and, unable to identify the specific herbs, decided to bring the entire mountain back to Lanka. After administering the medicines, he returned the mountain to its original place in the Himalayas.

Day 6

On the fifth night of battle, Sugreeva decided to launch a counterattack on Lanka. The Vanaras stormed the city in the night and set it on fire, intending to raze it completely. The terrified Rakshasas were taken by surprise as the Vanaras swiftly disappeared as they appeared. Furious, Ravana prepared for next day (6th day) and sent Kumbha and Nikumbha, the sons of Kumbhakarna, into battle. Hanuman engaged Nikumbha, severed his limbs, and eliminated Kumbha. Ravana then appointed Makaraksha to face Rama, but Makaraksha was no match for him. As the sixth day ended, Ravana turned once again to approach Indrajit to enter the battle on the seventh day.

Day 7

On the seventh day of battle, Indrajit, Ravana's son, used an illusion to deceive the Vanaras by creating a false image of Sita and appearing to kill her. This act plunged Rama and the Vanara army into despair. However, Vibhishana, Ravana's brother who had defected to Rama's side, quickly exposed the deception. He explained that Indrajit was using this tactic to buy time to perform a powerful ritual at the Nikumbala Devi shrine, which could make him invincible. Vibhishana urged the Vanaras to disrupt the ritual before it could be completed.

Lakshman, accompanied by the Vanaras, engaged Indrajit in a fierce battle near the shrine. Both warriors sustained severe injuries as the fight raged on into the night. In the climax of the battle, Lakshman invoked the Aindrastra, a divine weapon, and successfully severed Indrajit's head, thus eliminating Ravana's most formidable warrior. The Vanaras rejoiced, knowing they had defeated a significant threat. This victory not only marked the end of Indrajit's illusionary tactics but also symbolized the triumph over the ego's illusion of invincibility. Hanuman played a crucial role in supporting this effort, ensuring the success of the mission.

Day 8

On the eighth day of the battle, following the heavy losses and mourning in Lanka, the Rakshasas even started denouncing Ravana and Surpanakha. Ravana, with no one else to turn to, decided to join the battle himself. He fought fiercely, killing many Vanaras and directly engaging Rama. During the clash, Vibhishana attacked Ravana's horses, and Lakshman was injured by a spear while trying to save him.

Lakshman lay motionless, but Sushena assured that his breathing was stable, and Hanuman was again sent to the Himalayas to fetch healing herbs.

Ravana took a break and at that time Lord Indra appeared, gifting Rama a chariot. When Ravana returned Rama and Ravana engaged in their final battle. As Ravana's heads grew back each time they were severed, Rama recited the Aditya Hridayam Stotram given by Agastya Muni. Using a powerful arrow provided also by Agastya Muni, Rama pierced Ravana, finally bringing him down.

Delving Deeper....

... meaning of the war?

As a metaphor for the inner struggle of one's true divine nature against the forces that embody baser ego and sensory pursuits.

The Vanaras, unarmed yet powerful through their use of tree roots, stones, and sheer numbers, represent the myriad thoughts and emotions that strive to overcome the baser instincts born from ego and sensory desires. Their overwhelming numbers, described in the Valmiki Ramayana as crores, signify the countless thoughts that can swamp and eventually overpower negative tendencies. Despite their primitive tools, the Vanaras are effective, symbolizing how even simple, pure thoughts can be powerful when aligned with a higher purpose.

In the war, the individual combat is depicted as each Vanara leader braving the arrows and clubs of the Rakshasas. When coming close, they topple chariots and smash the Rakshasas to overpower them. Allegorically, this means the sensory apparatus is derailed, like it is uprooted, and the negative behaviour is knocked out. This backdrop of the war story illustrates how a person's higher thoughts and emotions can defeat the lower, instinctual tendencies, leading to personal growth and transformation.

Sugreeva, representing the emotional mind, and Hanuman, embodying the devotional mind, are completely aligned with Rama (the inner divine) and Sita (inherent faith). This alignment signifies how emotions and devotion, when directed towards a higher purpose, can help conquer the ego and sensory desires.

Ravana and Indrajit represent the ego, and the illusion of invincibility created by ego and sensory indulgences. Indrajit, who has even defeated the Lord of Nature (Indra), embodies the false sense of security they provide. Ravana's arrogance and sense of invulnerability are akin to the ego's dominance over the self, while Indrajit's use of illusions parallels the illusory nature of these powers. This false sense of superiority operates on the level of Maya (illusion), obscuring the true power of the divine Self and preventing an understanding of true nature.

Vibhishana symbolizes the power of self-control and restraint over the senses. By siding with Rama and ultimately becoming the king of Lanka, Vibhishana shows that self-control and restraint lead to a life of inner peace and harmony, the metaphorical "Rama Rajya" or ideal state of being.

10.8 Hanuman lifting the mountain to bring the Healing Herbs

In the Valmiki Ramayana, Hanuman made two crucial trips to the Dronagiri mountain, each with a different impact on the war.

First Trip:

After a fierce battle, many Vanara warriors, including Sugriva, Angada, Nila, and Jambavan, were seriously wounded. Jambavan, though injured, urged Hanuman to retrieve healing herbs from the Dronagiri mountain (Gandamadana) to save them. Hanuman successfully located the required Sanjivani herb (to revive) and brought it back to Lanka. The herbs healed the injured warriors, allowing them to rejoin the fight and boost the morale of Rama's army.

Second Trip:

The second trip occurred when Lakshman was severely wounded by Indrajit's arrow. This injury was life-threatening, and Sushena, the Vanara physician, prescribed four specific herbs to revive Lakshman: Mrita-Sanjivani (to revive), Vishalyakarani (to heal wounds), Savarni (to restore the body), and Sandhani (to repair fractures).

This time, unable to identify the herbs, Hanuman lifted the entire Dronagiri mountain and brought it to Lanka. The herbs revived Lakshman, restoring his strength and helping him return to battle.

Lakshman's recovery was crucial in turning the tide of the war, eventually leading to Rama's victory over Ravana. Afterward, Hanuman returned the mountain to its original place (told in some retellings) . This second mission demonstrated Hanuman's unparalleled strength and determination in ensuring victory for the forces of dharma.

... meaning of lifting the mountain

Hanuman's act of lifting the mountain can be viewed through an esoteric lens, symbolizing the transformative power of devotion in overcoming life's most difficult challenges.

When Lakshman, the embodiment of focus and discipline, is struck down by Indrajit's mystical weapon—representing the illusion of invincibility or the overwhelming obstacles in life—he is rendered unconscious. This state symbolizes how even focus and discipline can falter in the face of deep-rooted illusions or feelings of hopelessness.

At this critical moment, it is Hanuman, the personification of devotion and selfless service, who steps in to restore vitality. Hanuman's journey to the Dronagiri mountain represents the giant effort or mountain of spiritual resolve needed to heal and overcome obstacles in life. The herbs he retrieves (Sanjeevani and others) signify the power of divine grace and inner healing that restore Lakshman's focus and bring him back to life.

The entire episode serves as a powerful allegory that emphasizes how devotion (Bhakti) can literally move mountains. Through unwavering dedication and faith, Hanuman defies physical limitations, showing that when aligned with divine purpose, one can overcome any illusion (Maya) and bring about miraculous change. The message is clear: devotional power is the key to dispelling the deepest illusions and healing life's most serious wounds, restoring not only life but also spiritual balance.

In essence, Hanuman's journey to bring the Sanjeevani herb is a metaphor for the healing power of pure devotion, demonstrating how faith can lift even the heaviest burdens and restore light to the darkest of moments.

This story illustrates that no challenge is too great to surmount when one has faith, dedication, and devotion, ultimately dispelling the illusion of invincibility that stems from the ego or other negative tendencies. It teaches that devotional power has the strength to heal, uplift, and transform even in dire situations, restoring balance and leading the way to spiritual awakening.

10.9 Sage Agastya and the Aditya Hridaya Hymn

Sage Agastya in the Ramayana stands as a powerful embodiment of spiritual wisdom and inner calm, actively shaping the course of the epic, particularly during the climactic battle between Rama and Ravana.

Long before this final confrontation, in the dense Dandakaranya forest, Ravana, confident in his invincibility, arrogantly disturbed Sage Agastya during his meditation. Unfazed, Agastya cursed Ravana, predicting his downfall at the hands of a human—Rama. This curse was not just a rebuke but a divine decree, foreshadowing Ravana's eventual defeat and revealing the vulnerabilities in his seemingly unassailable power.

Years later, during Rama's exile, Agastya met him in the forest and, recognizing Rama's divine mission, provided him with sacred weapons—Vishnu's bow and arrows, a sword, and a quiver that never empties. These were not just tools of war but symbols of divine support, empowering Rama with the spiritual strength needed for his epic battle against darkness.

As the final battle with Ravana drained Rama's energy, Agastya reappeared, instructing him to chant the Aditya Hridaya, a powerful hymn dedicated to the Sun God. The recitation infused Rama with renewed strength and clarity, revitalizing him with divine energy. The Aditya Hridaya symbolized the ultimate source of light and knowledge, guiding Rama to overcome the darkness of doubt and fatigue.

Sage Agastya's contributions to the Ramayana are profound—his curse foretold Ravana's downfall, his gifts empowered Rama, and the Aditya Hridaya provided the spiritual energy needed for victory. Agastya's role highlights the importance of inner strength, divine guidance, and the ultimate triumph of light over darkness, serving as a testament to humility, balance, and unwavering commitment to dharma.

Chanting the Aditya Hridaya dispels doubt, fear, and negativity, offering peace and resilience. It helps align with higher ideals, cultivate inner strength, and find clarity amid modern life's complexities. In a world where external pressures can overwhelm, the Aditya Hridaya serves as a source of spiritual empowerment, reminding us that true victory and fulfilment come from within.

Learn to recite the Aditya Hridaya Stotra

https://www.youtube.com/watch?v=6oIrgLehqKA

The Mystical Aditya Hridaya

Both Rama and Ravana represent inner, nonphysical qualities within the human psyche—Rama embodying virtues such as righteousness, wisdom, true divine nature, and inner strength, while Ravana symbolizes baser aspects like ego, desire, and pride. Sage Agastya, acting as a spiritual guru, provides Rama with divine weapons that serve as metaphors for tools of inner purification, representing the spiritual power to cut through ignorance, overcome negative impulses, and achieve inner stillness.

The final encounter between Rama and Ravana in the Valmiki Ramayana is an allegory for the inner battle between higher consciousness and the lower self. As Rama confronts Ravana, it symbolizes the struggle between the enlightened self and the darker aspects of the mind. The Aditya Hridaya, chanted by Rama at Sage Agastya's behest, acts as a mystical invocation of the Sun, infusing Rama with divine energy, clarity, and strength, helping him transcend exhaustion.

In this allegorical battle, Rama's arrows—symbolizing focused thoughts—pierce through Ravana's ten heads, each representing a facet of ego, desire, and attachment. The final blow is delivered by Rama using the powerful Brahmastra, which he aimed directly at Ravana's heart, symbolizing the destruction of Ravana's core arrogance and pride. There is no specific mention in the Valmiki Ramayana of Vibhishana advising Rama to target Ravana's solar plexus, but it well be true, since it is related to Manipura chakra.

This act, empowered by the Aditya Hridaya, represents the triumph of the higher self over the lower self, where inner stillness and wisdom dispel the illusions of ego and desire, leading to spiritual evolution.

Practicing Manipura Chakra meditation is a way to engage in this inner battle, as it strengthens personal power, dismantles ego, and cultivates the inner clarity essential for spiritual growth. Deploying the Brahmastra symbolizes establishing a deep connection to divine energy, intense spiritual discipline, and precise intent, with the wielder maintaining unwavering focus and a keen awareness of its profound consequences.

Below is a version of the Aditya Hridaya to be used when chanting the Manipura Chakra meditation mantra, "Ram," enhancing its effects and benefiting from the mind-gut connection that modern science endorses.

https://www.youtube.com/watch?v=9XFCqaPlrn4&t=2s

10.10 The last rites of Ravana

After Ravana's death in the Valmiki Ramayana, the aftermath involves Rama addressing both the Vanaras and the Rakshasas, as well as offering guidance to Vibhishana.

Mandodari, Ravana's wife, laments over his body, expressing profound sorrow. She acknowledges his great power and lamentably notes how his arrogance and refusal to heed wise counsel led to his downfall. Her grief is a poignant reminder of the consequences of unchecked ambition and ego.

Rama addresses the Vanaras and Rakshasas, emphasizing the importance of moving forward with a sense of duty and compassion. He praises the Vanaras for their bravery and loyalty, acknowledging their crucial role in the victory. To the Rakshasas, he extends a message of reconciliation, urging them to abandon their enmity and embrace a future of peace under Vibhishana's rule.

Initially, Vibhishana is reluctant to perform the funeral rites for Ravana, viewing him as an enemy. However, Rama advises him on the importance of honouring the dead, irrespective of their actions. He emphasizes that duty and compassion should transcend personal animosities. Rama's guidance helps Vibhishana see the value in performing his brother's last rites, which signifies the importance of familial duty and respect for life, even in the face of past wrongdoings.

Rama's words to the gathered forces are filled with wisdom and a call for unity:

- To the Vanaras: He expresses his deep gratitude for their unwavering support and bravery. He recognizes their sacrifices and valor, highlighting how their collective effort and loyalty led to the defeat of Ravana.

- To the Rakshasas: Rama urges them to forsake their past enmity and embrace peace. He assures them that under Vibhishana's rule, there will be justice and prosperity. He speaks of the futility of hatred and the benefits of unity and harmony.

Delving Deeper....

The story (Katha Yuktham) illustrates the internal battle- the facts (Purva Yuktham) are the strife that everyone faces between their higher self and their lower, ego-driven tendencies. The Vanaras' actions, though seemingly chaotic, represent the persistent effort of the mind to uproot deeply ingrained beliefs and habits.

Sugreeva and Hanuman's roles highlight the importance of aligning emotions and devotion with a higher purpose. This alignment transforms these powerful forces as allies against the ego and sensory desires.

Vibhishana's ascension to the throne signifies that true mastery over oneself leads to a state of inner peace and governance. A "new Lanka" or ideal state of being is achieved through self-discipline and restraint.

The Valmiki Ramayana, through its layered narrative, offers profound insights into the human psyche and the eternal struggle between the higher self and lower instincts. By understanding these allegories, young adults can gain valuable guidance on leading a life of self-control, devotion, and alignment with inner divine wisdom, ultimately achieving their own "Rama Rajya." This deeper reflection encourages a life of purpose beyond mere sensory pursuits, fostering true personal growth and fulfilment.

In the Valmiki Ramayana, Ravana is depicted as a figure driven by ego, desire, and unchecked ambition, leading to his ultimate downfall. He is not portrayed as the composer of the Shiva Tandava Stotram nor as a tragic hero. While his intelligence and power are acknowledged, his moral failings are the focus, overshadowing any redeeming qualities or spiritual devotion.

After Ravana's death on the battlefield, Rama's reaction is not simply one of triumph. Instead, recognizing Ravana's strategic brilliance and effective governance, Rama urges Lakshman to learn from him. He tells Lakshman to approach Ravana, not just as a vanquished enemy but as a wise ruler who can still impart valuable lessons on leadership and governance. Despite Ravana's flaws, Rama acknowledges the wisdom he possessed, particularly in managing alliances and ruling Lanka. This reflects Rama's deep understanding of leadership, where he emphasizes the need to learn from all experiences, even those with adversaries.

By encouraging Lakshman to approach Ravana, Rama demonstrates humility and a broader perspective on the complexity of human nature. He understands that even someone like Ravana, with all his moral failures, can still offer valuable lessons. Rama's gesture underscores the importance of lifelong learning and the idea that true wisdom often comes from unexpected sources. This act reflects Rama's ability to transcend the simple dichotomy of good and evil, offering a nuanced view of leadership, knowledge, and growth.

Note

In the Valmiki Ramayana, there is no direct mention of Rama asking Lakshman to learn from Ravana after his death. This episode appears in later versions like the Ramcharitmanas and other regional retellings. In these, Rama advises Lakshman to seek wisdom from Ravana, emphasizing the value of learning even from one's enemies, particularly in matters of governance and strategy. However, this scene is absent from the original text by Valmiki.

Mandodari's Lament

"Oh Ravana, my king, my husband... how has it come to this? You, who were so mighty and wise, lay fallen and silent. Your quest for power, your defiance of the divine, has brought us to these dark days. I warned you, my love, of the peril in desiring Sita, a woman of such celestial bond with her husband, Rama. Yet, your pride, your indomitable will, blinded you to any counsel.

You, the great scholar, versed in the Vedas and a devotee of Shiva, how could you stray so far from dharma? Each decision you made, driven by ambition and desire, led us further into the shadows. Now, Lanka weeps, and I, your queen, am left to mourn not just you but the peace and prosperity of our kingdom that was.

Was it worth it, my lord? The war, the destruction, the lives lost... all for a fleeting victory that you sought against the ordained? Here I stand, lamenting over your body, surrounded by the ruin of our realm. Oh, how I wish you had chosen a different path, one that led not to glory and power but to righteousness and wisdom.

But even now, in this hour of despair, I remember you not just for the choices that doomed us but also for the moments of love and strength that bonded us. Rest now, my king, for your battles are over. I pray that your journey onward is free of the burdens that weighed you down in this life."

Through her lament, Mandodari not only grieves for Ravana but also articulates a critical reflection on his life choices, highlighting the tragic consequences of his actions on himself and their kingdom.

Ravana's curses

In the Uttara Kanda of the Valmiki Ramayana, the curses of Vedavati and Nalakubara play pivotal roles in shaping Ravana's actions towards Sita.

Vedavati's Curse: Ravana attempted to molest Vedavati, a woman destined for Lord Vishnu. In her resistance, she cursed Ravana, declaring that her reincarnation would bring about his downfall. This curse is seen as fulfilled through Sita, considered Vedavati's reincarnation, leading to Ravana's destruction.

Nalakubara's Curse: After Ravana assaulted Rambha, who was betrothed to Nalakubara (Kubera's son), Nalakubara cursed Ravana, stating that if he ever violated a woman against her will, his head would explode. This curse prevented Ravana from physically harming Sita, forcing him to try to woo her through persuasion during her captivity.

These curses underscore divine retribution while revealing that Ravana's adherence to restraint was motivated more by fear of personal consequences than by moral integrity. This deepens the complexity of his character and the theme of moral choices in the Ramayana.

Chapter 11

War is Over...the Return to Ayodhya... Rama Rajya

11.1 Coronation of Vibhishana .... The Agni Pareeksha...

Following the last rites of Ravana, the battlefield's tension turned into a solemn reflection. Vibhishana was crowned the new king of Lanka, bringing a sense of hope and renewal to the once dark kingdom. With the ashes of war still settling, Rama sent for Sita, setting the stage for a pivotal moment.

As Sita approached, a profound silence fell over the gathered Vanaras, Rakshasas, and loyal companions. Rama, his face stern yet composed, addressed Sita with a heavy heart. "Sita," he began, his voice firm but laden with sorrow, "You have endured great suffering and shown unwavering virtue. Yet, for the honour of our lineage and to quell any doubt, you must undergo the Agni Pareeksha and prove your purity."

Sita, her eyes reflecting both pain and determination, replied, "My Lord, I understand the necessity of this trial. Let the fire god himself testify to my purity."

With resolve, Sita walked towards the blazing fire, her head held high, fully adorned as Rama wanted her to be. The crowd watched in anguished silence as she entered the flames.

The fire roared around her, but she remained unscathed, her serene face glowing with divine radiance. Agni, the fire god, emerged from the flames, holding Sita in his arms. "Rama," Agni declared, his voice thunderous, "Sita is pure and untainted. She has proven her virtue beyond all doubt."

Rama's stern expression softened into relief and joy. He stepped forward, taking Sita's hand from Agni. "Sita," he said, his voice filled with warmth, "You have proven your purity and strength. Your unwavering faith and virtue have silenced all doubts. You are my true and rightful queen."

The assembly erupted in cheers. Hanuman's eyes filled with tears of joy, and Lakshman smiled proudly. The Vanaras and Rakshasas rejoiced, celebrating the vindication of Sita and the restoration of honour.

Amidst this joyous moment, Indra, the king of the gods, descended from the heavens. "Rama," he announced, "As a boon for your unparalleled devotion and righteousness, I shall restore all the fallen Vanaras to life." With a divine gesture, Indra brought the fallen Vanaras back to life, their injuries healed, and their strength renewed.

Explaining Rama requiring Agni Pareeksha

Sita's Agni Pareeksha is one of the most emotionally charged and symbolically rich moments in the Ramayana. This trial by fire, orchestrated by Rama, holds profound significance in terms of honour, truth, and the triumph of virtue over doubt and suspicion.

The context of the Agni Pareeksha lies in the aftermath of Rama's victory over Ravana and the liberation of Sita from her captivity in Lanka. Despite Rama's deep love and unwavering faith in Sita, he recognizes the necessity to uphold the honour and trust of his people. Rama's decision to subject Sita to the trial was not born out of personal doubt but from his duty as a king to ensure that the purity of his queen was beyond reproach, visible to the entire world.

As Rama requests Sita to prepare for the Agni Pareeksha, he asks her to dress in her finest attire. This request underscores his respect and love for her, highlighting her dignity and nobility as his queen, regardless of the ordeal she had endured. Sita's unwavering resolve to undergo the trial illustrates her strength, virtue, and unshakeable devotion to Rama. Her willingness to step into the flames is a testament to her purity and the deep trust she has in her own righteousness and in Rama's love.

The divine intervention of Agni, the god of fire, adds a celestial dimension to the event. As Sita steps into the flames, Agni rises to protect her, unharmed and unblemished, further endorsing her purity and honour. This divine affirmation not only vindicates Sita but also serves to silence any remaining doubts among the people of Ayodhya.

Moreover, the involvement of Indra, who grants a boon to restore the lives of the fallen Vanaras, symbolizes the restoration of balance and righteousness. This act of divine benevolence highlights the cosmic justice at play and underscores the gods' endorsement of Sita's virtue and Rama's rightful actions.

In essence, the Agni Pareeksha was essential for demonstrating to the world the unassailable purity and virtue of Sita. It was a ritual of cosmic and social validation, ensuring that her honour was upheld in the eyes of all. The episode, filled with emotional intensity and divine interventions, enriches the narrative, making it deeply engaging and impactful. It encapsulates themes of honour, purity, and the triumph of truth, reinforcing the moral victory of Rama and Sita and the restoration of dharma.

This portrayal enhances the emotional depth and narrative richness of the Ramayana, making the Agni Pareeksha a pivotal moment that resonates with the values of righteousness, duty, and divine justice.

11.2 Return to Ayodhya

After Sita's successful Agni Pareeksha, the atmosphere in Lanka was one of relief and jubilation. With the assurance of Sita's purity and honour restored, preparations began for their return to Ayodhya. Rama, Sita, Lakshman, and their loyal companions boarded the divine Pushpaka Vimana, a magnificent aerial chariot that could travel at incredible speeds.

Rama, Sita, Lakshman, and Hanuman, along with the Vanara leaders Sugreeva, Angada, Jambavan, and others, embarked on the Pushpaka Vimana. This celestial chariot, gifted by Kubera and now in the possession of Vibhishana, had the ability to expand and accommodate everyone comfortably. They visited important places so that Sita also understood their journey during her period of abduction.

Kishkindha: They made a brief stop to bid farewell to the Vanaras' homeland and to thank them for their invaluable assistance in the battle against Ravana.

Pampa Lake: They visited Pampa Lake, where Rama reminisced about the time he spent there searching for Sita and his meeting with Shabari.

Rishyamuka Mountain: They recalled Rama's first meeting with Hanuman and Sugreeva, which led to the formation of their alliance.

Sita, recognizing the immense contribution of the Vanaras, requested that their wives be included in the celebrations. She believed that their presence would honour the sacrifices made by the Vanaras and ensure a complete and joyous coronation.

Bharadwaja's Ashram: They visited the sage Bharadwaja's ashram near Prayag (the Ganga Jamuna Confluence), seeking his blessings for their return journey.

The Pushpaka Vimana then headed towards Nandigram, where Bharata had been living a life of austerity, ruling Ayodhya in Rama's stead. Hanuman had flown ahead to inform Bharata of Rama's imminent return, ensuring he was prepared for the joyous reunion.

Hanuman delivered the news to Bharata, who had been waiting patiently for Rama's return. Overwhelmed with joy, Bharata prepared a grand welcome for his beloved brother.

As the Pushpaka Vimana descended in Nandigram, Bharata rushed to greet Rama, Lakshman, and Sita with tears of happiness. The brothers embraced each other, and Bharata returned the sandals he had been keeping on the throne as a symbol of Rama's authority.

11.3 Coronation and Rama Rajya

Upon arriving at Nandigram, Rama and Sita were greeted by an emotional and ecstatic Bharata. Bharata, who had been living a life of austerity and ruling Ayodhya admirably in Rama's stead, rushed to meet his brother. Falling at Rama's feet, Bharata exclaimed, "My dear brother, you have returned! Ayodhya will now shine with your presence."

Rama lifted the prostrated Bharata and embraced him warmly, saying, "Brother, Rise. You have carried the burden of the kingdom with great devotion and honour. Your sacrifices and faith have kept our family's legacy alive."

The reunion was heartfelt, with tears of joy and relief flowing freely. Rama, Lakshman, and Sita were moved by Bharata's unwavering devotion. Rama then took back the sandals that Bharata had kept on the throne as a symbol of his authority.

Bharata, in his chariot, led the grand procession back to Ayodhya. Rama, Sita, Lakshman, Hanuman, and the Vanaras were all part of this magnificent return. As they entered Ayodhya, the streets were lined with citizens cheering, singing, and showering flowers. The entire city was decorated, and the atmosphere was filled with joy and celebration.

The Vanaras, who had played a crucial role in the battle against Ravana, were given great respect and honour. Sita's request to include the Vanara wives in the celebration added to the festivity, highlighting the unity and gratitude among Rama's allies.

The coronation ceremony was held with great splendour. Sage Vashistha, the royal priest, conducted the rituals. He placed the crown on Rama's head, officially anointing him as the king of Ayodhya. Sita stood beside him, adorned as the queen. The citizens of Ayodhya rejoiced, knowing that Rama's reign would bring peace and prosperity.

Vibhishana, now the king of Lanka, was also honoured for his loyalty and righteousness.

With the ceremonies concluded, the visitors from Kishkindha and Lanka returned to their homelands, carrying with them the blessings and gratitude of Ayodhya.

Rama's rule, known as Rama Rajya, began to the delight of all citizens. His reign was marked by justice, peace, and prosperity, not only in Ayodhya but also in the allied kingdoms of Lanka and Kishkindha.

This grand return and coronation symbolized the triumph of divine over profane and the establishment of a righteous and just rule in all the three kingdoms. Rama's leadership, Sita as Queen supported by his loyal allies, brought about a golden age, reflecting the ideals of dharma and the importance of unity and devotion.

Delving Deeper....

The journey back to Ayodhya in the Valmiki Ramayana symbolizes a young adult's growth and maturity. Rama's return reflects on past trials, emphasizing the importance of learning from challenges that shape character and wisdom. It highlights the value of gratitude for the support received along the way.

Rama's coronation represents success, but it also underscores the need for humility and respect. Like Rama, acknowledge those who supported you, showing appreciation as success is rarely achieved alone. His reign, Rama Rajya, symbolizes peace, prosperity, and justice, reflecting the benefits of a life free from ego and unethical desires.

In essence, Rama's journey and coronation teach the importance of self-reflection, controlling ego, and living ethically. By embracing humility, gratitude, and higher ideals, one can lead a fulfilling and harmonious life.

Rama Rajya, his reign, symbolizes peace, prosperity, and justice. Similarly, a life free from ego and unethical desires creates an environment of joy and harmony. By embracing respect, humility, and gratitude, your actions can foster a community of trust and happiness.

In essence, Rama's return to Ayodhya and his coronation highlights personal growth and ethical living. This journey encourages self-reflection, gratitude, and the pursuit of higher ideals, leading to a fulfilling and harmonious life.

The Heart of Devotion

During the grand royal gathering, Rama and Sita were bestowing gifts upon their loyal allies. When it was Hanuman's turn, Rama offered him a necklace of precious pearls. But Hanuman, ever the humble devotee, began breaking each pearl between his teeth, searching intently within. The onlookers, puzzled, questioned his actions. Hanuman calmly explained that he was seeking Rama and Sita within the pearls, as he believes that anything of true value must contain the essence of the divine couple.

Doubt rippled through the crowd, challenging his devotion. In response, Hanuman took a bold and dramatic step. With unwavering resolve, he tore open his chest, revealing his heart. To everyone's astonishment, there, enthroned within his heart, were the images of Rama and Sita.

This awe-inspiring act silenced the sceptics, proving that his love and devotion were so profound that the divine couple literally resided within him. For Hanuman, Rama and Sita were not just deities to be worshipped—they were the very essence of his being, eternally alive in his heart.

Chapter 12

The Last Phase – Sita's Return to Earth... Rama, Lava and Kusha

12.1 Sita Banishment.... Lava Kusha ... Valmiki and Sita's
   return to earth

After his coronation, Rama's rule brought unparalleled prosperity and peace to Ayodhya. His reign, known as Rama Rajya, was characterized by justice, compassion, and righteousness. Under Rama's leadership, the kingdom thrived, with citizens living in harmony and contentment. Law and order were maintained, and there was no poverty or suffering. Sita, as the queen, played a significant role in upholding the moral and ethical standards of the court. The couple's happiness grew when Sita became pregnant, bringing additional joy to the people of Ayodhya as they anticipated the birth of their future heirs.

However, rumours and discontentment arose among the citizens of Ayodhya, questioning Sita's purity due to her time in Lanka. Despite having no personal doubt about Sita's fidelity, Rama, as a ruler, feels compelled to address the public's concerns to maintain the integrity of his reign.

Rama makes the heart-wrenching decision to leave Sita near the hermitage of sage Valmiki, who offers her shelter and support. Sita gives birth to twin sons, Lava and Kusha, in the ashram, and they grow up under Valmiki's care. Valmiki educates the boys in various arts and sciences and teaches them to recite the epic Ramayana, which he has just composed.

Years later, during a grand festival in Ayodhya, Lava and Kusha recite the Ramayana in Rama's court. Rama is moved by the narration, which includes details he had not yet lived through. This prompts him to invite the boys, along with Valmiki and Sita, to Ayodhya. It is revealed that Lava and Kusha are his sons, bringing a mix of joy and sorrow to the reunion.

In a final attempt to prove her purity beyond any doubt, Sita responds to Rama's request to come to Ayodhya, but she calls upon Mother Earth to take her back if she has remained pure. With unwavering faith, Sita steps forward and invokes her mother, Bhumi Devi, to attest to her innocence. In a dramatic and divine response, the ground splits open, and a radiant throne emerges from the earth. Sita, exuding grace and serenity, is welcomed onto the throne by Mother Earth herself. As the ground closes, Sita is taken back into the earth, signifying her untainted purity and marking the end of her mortal life. This poignant moment underscores the depth of Sita's virtue and the divine acknowledgment of her unwavering fidelity and righteousness.

Lava and Kusha are accepted into the royal family and continue to live with Rama. They grow up to be valorous and wise, embodying the virtues and legacy of their parents. The epic continues with Rama ruling Ayodhya justly and continuing the lineage of the Ikshvaku dynasty, however sad he was.

Delving Deeper....

In the profound metaphor for the spiritual journey of an individual who has established control over ego and senses, Sita's banishment appears inconsistent.

The doubts arise during Sita's pregnancy, the arrival of progeny and the continuation of one's legacy. However, the citizens of Ayodhya, questioning Sita's purity due to her time in Lanka and the incident with the golden deer having fallen to the fleeting attraction, represent societal doubts and pressures regarding the purity and worthiness of one's future offspring.

Rama's decision to banish Sita, despite his personal faith in her purity, reflects the inevitable compromises even a realized individual must make in response to external societal pressures. This act illustrates the tension between inner conviction and societal expectations. Rama, embodying the ideal ruler, feels compelled to address the concerns of his people to maintain their trust and ensure the stability of his kingdom.

In this context, Sita's banishment is not just a personal sacrifice but a symbolic act of prioritizing the greater good over personal beliefs. It highlights the harsh reality that even those who are spiritually advanced may face situations where they must compromise their own faith and values to uphold societal norms and responsibilities, especially when considering the future well-being of their community or legacy.

Lava and Kusha

Their upbringing in Valmiki's ashram, isolated from society and under the guidance of a sage, symbolizes the nurturing of pure, untainted potential within a protected environment. This setting allows them to develop a deep understanding of their purpose and heritage, akin to an individual's inner growth away from societal influences.

Valmiki's composition of the Ramayana during Sita's pregnancy in confinement underscores the idea that children, even before birth, come with an intrinsic connection to their life's purpose. Lava and Kusha's recitation of the Ramayana to Rama symbolizes the reinforcement of spiritual lessons and the eternal quest to overcome ego and achieve emotional and devotional alignment. This interaction highlights how, even when one has led a life with compromised inner beliefs due to external pressures, the next generation can revive and reinforce these spiritual values.

Rama's acceptance of Lava and Kusha signifies the joy and fulfilment that family and progeny bring, despite personal sacrifices and compromises. Their presence and the propagation of the Ramayana through their recitation demonstrate that the spiritual journey is perpetuated and enriched by the next generation. Sita's return to Mother Earth symbolizes the culmination of her earthly trials and the ongoing nature of life's spiritual narrative through her children.

Lava and Kusha's recital of the remaining part of the Ramayana, particularly the UttaraKand, only after Sita's departure, signifies that the full scope of spiritual wisdom and life's trials becomes clear through reflection and the contributions of subsequent generations. This narrative highlight that faith and spiritual quests are ongoing, transcending individual lives and manifesting through the stories and actions of descendants. It emphasizes the cyclical nature of spiritual growth and the reinforcement of core values through family and legacy, teaching that true understanding and wisdom are often realized through the lens of time and the continuity of life's teachings.

Valmiki and Sita's return to earth

Valmiki's reflection on the separation of the Krauncha birds at the beginning of the Ramayana mirrors the profound separation of Rama and Sita. This separation, filled with pain and longing, resonates throughout the epic, symbolizing the universal sorrow of separation and the inevitable trials that accompany love and duty.

As the epic nears its conclusion, Valmiki's role becomes even more significant. The sage, who has been the chronicler of this divine tale, plays a crucial part in the dramatic return of Sita to Ayodhya. This moment marks a poignant turning point, where Rama finally embraces his sons, Lava and Kusha. Their acceptance signifies not only the reconciliation of past pains but also the continuity of life through the next generation. It is a powerful testament to the enduring nature of family bonds and the healing power of acceptance.

In a grand assembly filled with the citizens of Ayodhya, sages, and the royal court, Sita stands poised, her presence commanding attention. As she prepares to speak, the air is thick with anticipation.

"People of Ayodhya," Sita begins, her voice steady and resonant, "I have walked the path of dharma and endured trials that tested the very essence of my being. My journey has been one of love, sacrifice, and unwavering devotion. Today, I stand before you, not to seek validation, but to reaffirm the purity of my heart and the truth that has guided my steps."

Her eyes, filled with a mixture of sorrow and strength, scan the crowd. "Rama, my lord and the king, has fulfilled his duty to his people, even when it demanded the greatest personal sacrifice. My trials were not merely my own; they were a testament to the values we hold dear—honour, loyalty, and righteousness."

The audience is captivated, the weight of her words sinking in. "Lava and Kusha, our sons, embody the future of Ayodhya, a future built on the foundations of truth and virtue. May their reign be one of peace, prosperity, and adherence to dharma."

Suddenly, the ground beneath Sita begins to tremble softly, and the air fills with a gentle, soothing hum. The audience watches in awe as the Earth herself, Bhumi devi, begins to rise, her form emerging from the soil with an ethereal glow. She is resplendent, her presence exuding warmth and maternal grace.

"My beloved daughter," Bhumi devi 's voice resonates with a serene power, "you have endured much, and your purity and devotion have never wavered. It is time for you to return to your true home."

Bhumi devi turns to the assembled crowd, her gaze encompassing all. "Witness, people of Ayodhya, the virtue and sacrifice of Sita. She has upheld dharma in the face of great adversity, and her spirit is untarnished."

Rama, standing beside his sons, looks upon the scene with a mixture of sorrow and reverence. He steps forward, his voice filled with emotion. "Mother Earth, I have always known Sita's purity. Her trials were not a test for me, but for the world to see her unwavering virtue."

Bhumi devi nods, her eyes full of understanding. "Rama, your journey has been one of great sacrifice as well. The time has come for the world to understand the true essence of your union and the principles you have both upheld."

As Bhumi devi gently takes Sita's hand, the ground opens, revealing a path illuminated by divine light. Sita turns to Rama, her eyes conveying a final message of love and devotion. "Our love and duty have been witnessed by the world. My journey here is complete, but my spirit will always be with you."

With a final, graceful step, Sita follows Bhumi devi i into the Earth, their forms gradually merging with the light until they are no longer visible. The ground closes softly, leaving the crowd in a state of reverent silence.

Rama's reign, with a golden statue of Sita beside him, underscores the eternal presence of her spirit. This symbolic gesture highlights the enduring nature of their bond and the perpetual impact of profound connections.

This cycle of separation and reunion reflects the ongoing nature of life's spiritual quest. It underscores that even for a realized individual or a divine incarnation, life is far from a paradise. The Uttara Ramayana illustrates the continuous journey of growth, learning, and adaptation to the complexities of existence. It reminds us that life involves enduring compromises and navigating through challenges, but also finding strength in faith, love, and the divine essence within.

Valmiki not only brings closure to the epic tale but also provides a profound lesson on the human condition. The story of Rama and Sita, with its themes of love, loss, and reunion, serves as a timeless reminder of the spiritual journey we all undertake. It emphasizes that despite the trials and tribulations we face, the quest for spiritual fulfilment and the bonds we form along the way are what give life its deepest meaning.

12.2 Shambuka Vadha

In Valmiki Ramayana's Uttara Kanda, the story of Shambuka highlights the complexities of dharma, individual aspirations and societal norms during Rama's reign, in Treta Yuga.

The narrative unfolds when an untimely death of a young brahmin boy leads Rama to seek the cause of this disturbance to his rule. Guided by Sage Narada, Rama learns that the disruption is caused by a Shudra, named Shambuka, who is performing severe penances with the aim to ascend to heaven in his mortal form and become a celestial being - a privilege reserved for certain varnas in that era. Narada clarifies that in the Satya, Treta and Dwapara Yugas, only certain varnas (social classes) are permitted to perform penances to become preceptors and reach higher orders, specifically Brahmins, Kshatriyas, and Vaishyas in Treta Yuga.

Rama finds Shambuka doing penance in an upside-down posture and questions him:

Rama: "Shambuka, what is the purpose of your penance?"

Shambuka: "My lord, I wish to ascend to the heavens in this very body, to become a celestial being."

Rama, bound by the dharma of his times, explains that such practices are against the cosmic order in Treta Yuga. Despite Shambuka's aspirations, Rama is compelled to uphold the social and cosmic laws of the period, leading to Shambuka's elimination, which is controversial but depicted as necessary for restoring the natural order and the boy's life applicable at that time.

This episode, often cited for its controversial nature, reflects the stringent varna system of that era contrasting sharply with the more inclusive spirit of Kali Yuga, where spiritual opportunities are accessible to all regardless of social class (ie free of any limitations)

Kali Yuga is the final age in Hindu cosmology, marked by moral decay, increased strife, and diminished righteousness, yet offering opportunities for personal spiritual growth through devotion and good deeds. In Kali Yuga, there will rise false preceptors and gurus, but through self-purification, any individual can evolve.

The story of Shambuka in the Uttara Kand and that of Trishanku in earlier Bala Kand showcase two instances of individuals seeking to ascend to heaven in their mortal forms, both of which confront the prevailing social and cosmic orders of their times and illustrates the limitations of human desires.

Trishanku was a king from the Solar Dynasty, an ancestor of Rama, who desired to ascend to heaven in his bodily form. Despite his royal status, the sages he approached initially refused to perform the necessary rites, as the idea of ascending to heaven in one's mortal body contradicted the existing cosmic laws. Eventually, Sage Vishwamitra, driven by his own ambitions to showcase his spiritual power, took on the challenge. Despite numerous obstacles and the initial opposition of the gods, Vishwamitra eventually creates a "new heaven" for Trishanku, where he remains suspended upside down.

Trishanku's eternal suspension between the heavens and the earth symbolizes the risks of defying one's destined path, often leading to unresolved consequences.

In a similar vein, Shambuka's breach of societal norms by pursuing severe ascetic practices not sanctioned for his varna underscores the conflict between personal spiritual goals and the societal rules of Treta Yuga.

Both narratives reflect the complex interplay between personal ambition and the overarching cosmic order, illustrating the repercussions of challenging established dharma, with Trishanku facing a perpetual limbo and Shambuka facing dire consequences.

The stories of Valmiki and Shambuka from the Valmiki Ramayana present contrasting paths within the same societal constraints. Valmiki, originally a hunter and said to be of Shudra origin, transformed into a revered sage through penance and divine intervention, eventually composing the Ramayana. His journey from a lower caste to a sage highlights the transformative power of spiritual enlightenment in ancient India.

Shambuka's tale, on the other hand, serves as a poignant narrative about the rigid societal norms of his time. As a Shudra, Shambuka undertook severe penance aiming for celestial ascension, an aspiration deemed inappropriate for his varna during the Treta Yuga. His actions were seen as a breach of dharma according to the societal laws of that era, which ultimately led to his elimination by Rama, enforcing the norms of dharma. This story underscores the limitations placed on spiritual practices based on varna, contrasting sharply with Valmiki's story of redemption and acceptance.

It should be noted that the varna system in Hinduism originally categorized society based on individual proclivities and duties, though it later merged with the rigid caste system (jati), often limiting social roles based on birth.

Both narratives explore the theme of rebirth and spiritual aspiration. While Valmiki's transformation is celebrated as a triumph of personal evolution, Shambuka's story is a tragic reminder of the harsh boundaries imposed by the ancient varna system. It is suggested that aspirations like those of Shambuka for immortality or celestial living without the requisite spiritual maturity or societal sanction were not only frowned upon but were also considered dangerous.

Valmiki's story did not end with his transformation into a sage; it continued to inspire as he shared his wisdom through the Ramayana. Though there's no mention of Valmiki's reincarnation, the cyclical nature of birth, death, and rebirth in Hindu philosophy might suggest that his soul would continue its journey, potentially influencing generations in new forms.

12.3 The Visit of Lord Kala and Lakshman's Banishment

The episode involving Lord Kala and Lakshman's subsequent banishment is one of the most poignant moments in the Ramayana, highlighting the complexities of dharma. Lord Kala's visit to Rama signifies the imminent conclusion of Rama's earthly duties as an avatar. Rama instructs Lakshman to guard their meeting, emphasizing the importance of privacy, even under the threat of severe consequences for any disturbance.

Lakshman, ever loyal, is placed in a moral quandary when Sage Durvasa arrives, a revered yet notoriously short-tempered sage, demanding immediate access to Rama. Caught between obeying his brother's strict orders and the potential disaster of offending a powerful sage, Lakshman chooses to prevent a curse by allowing Durvasa to enter. This decision leads to Lakshman breaching Rama's command, placing Rama in a position where he must uphold dharma by adhering to his word, even at great personal cost.

Rama's decision to banish Lakshman, while heartrending, reaffirms his unwavering dedication to dharma. This episode not only stresses the sacrifices inherent in adhering to dharma but also illustrates the tragic nature of such adherence, which often demands personal losses and emotional distress.

Lakshman's acceptance of his fate and his departure to the Sarayu River, where he ends his earthly existence, encapsulate the theme of duty and sacrifice. By entering the river, Lakshman returns to his divine form, Ananta Shesha, thus completing his role in this avatar and preparing to support Vishnu in future incarnations. This narrative emphasizes the cyclical nature of life and death and the profound spiritual underpinnings of Hindu philosophy.

Lakshman's banishment marks the end of his earthly duties, symbolizing his readiness to return to divine form. This event demonstrates the profound sacrifices inherent in upholding dharma and the need to relinquish earthly roles for spiritual progress. As an incarnation of Shesha, the cosmic serpent, Lakshman's life cycle contributes to cosmic order, emphasizing the transitory nature of avatars.

These divine incarnations restore balance and then recede, paving the way for new cycles. This process highlights the continuous divine intervention and the eternal cycle of life, underscoring that through ages, wisdom overcomes ignorance and light conquers darkness.

"Whenever there is a decline in righteousness and an increase in unrighteousness, O descendant of Bharata, at that time I manifest myself on earth. To protect the righteous, to annihilate the wicked, and to reestablish the principles of dharma, I appear age after age."

Lord Krishna - Bhagavat Gita Ch 4, verse 8

12.4 The End of Rama's Avatar

Yada yada hi dharmasya glanir bhavati Bharata,

abhyutthanam adharmasya tadatmanam srijamy aham.

Paritranaya sadhunam vinasaya cha duskritam,

dharmasamsthapanarthaya sambhavami yuge yuge."

Lord Krishna - Bhagavat Gita Ch 4, verse 8

The Final Chapter of Rama's Earthly Journey

As the divine drama of Lord Rama's avatar approaches its conclusion, the atmosphere in Ayodhya is charged with a sense of both fulfilment and poignant anticipation. Rama, ever the righteous and foresighted ruler, ensures the continuity and stability of his kingdom by appointing his twin sons, Lava and Kusha, as the future rulers of Ayodhya. Their upbringing in the hermitage of Sage Valmiki has prepared them for this significant responsibility, embodying the virtues and wisdom necessary to lead their people.

With the future of Ayodhya secure, Rama turns his attention to his own impending departure from the mortal realm. He understands that his mission on earth, to establish dharma and eradicate adharma, is complete. It is now time for him to return to his divine abode. This realization is not merely an acceptance of the end but a fulfilment of a divine cycle that he has played a crucial role in.

Rama, guided by a divine calling, proceeds to the banks of the sacred Sarayu River. Word of his departure spreads quickly, and a multitude of citizens, along with sages, ministers, and beings from various realms, gather to witness this profound event. Their hearts are heavy with the impending separation, yet they are filled with reverence and gratitude for the life and lessons imparted by their beloved king.

As Rama reaches the river, he offers his final salutations to the sacred waters and to the divine forces that have guided his journey. In a deeply symbolic act, he enters the Sarayu River, signifying the shedding of his mortal coil. As he immerses himself in the waters, Rama transcends his human form, revealing his true divine essence as Lord Vishnu, the preserver of the universe.

This moment of transformation is not just the end of an era but a powerful reminder of the eternal truths of Sanatana Dharma. Rama's departure illustrates the cyclical nature of life, death, and rebirth, a fundamental concept in Hindu philosophy. It underscores the idea that while mortal existence is transient, the principles of dharma and the divine presence are eternal.

The citizens of Ayodhya, witnessing this divine occurrence, are filled with a sense of awe and a deep understanding of the impermanence of life. They are reminded that while earthly roles and relationships are fleeting, the essence of dharma, righteousness, and divine duty transcends all.

Rama's return to his divine form signifies the restoration of cosmic order and the balance of the universe. It reaffirms the belief that the divine manifests in human form to guide and protect, but ultimately, all forms are transient, and the essence of the divine is eternal and unchanging.

In this profound conclusion to his earthly journey, Rama leaves behind a legacy that continues to inspire and guide generations. His life is a testament to the power of righteousness, the importance of fulfilling one's duties, and the ultimate transcendence of the soul.

Summary of Avatars' Final Acts in Uttarakhand

Lakshman: After inadvertently offending Sage Durvasa, Lakshman chooses to end his life in the Sarayu River, demonstrating his unwavering devotion and adherence to Rama's command, reflecting his commitment to his divine duty.

Bharata: Following Rama's departure, Bharata joins him by entering the Sarayu River, showcasing his dedication to his brother and the principles of dharma.

Shatrughna: After his brothers' departures, Shatrughna also enters the Sarayu River, maintaining his deep familial bonds and commitment. He previously ruled Mathura, setting the stage for the narrative of Krishna in the subsequent yuga.

Hanuman: Granted immortality, Hanuman remains on Earth, continuing his service by spreading Rama's teachings and assisting mankind, embodying eternal devotion.

Sugreeva: After a period of rule, Sugreeva passes on his kingdom to his successor and embraces a hermit's life, eventually leaving the earthly realm in emulation of Rama's renunciation.

Vibhishana: Blessed with longevity by Rama, Vibhishana continues to rule Lanka with justice and virtue, upholding the dharma instilled by Rama.

This summary captures the end-of-life journeys of key figures, highlighting their commitment to dharma and reflecting the cyclical nature of existence as portrayed in Hindu philosophy through the main avatars and their associates

In the Ramayana, the end of key characters, excluding Hanuman and Vibhishana, underscores life's impermanence and the eternal cycle of dharma, birth and death

Rama's departure marks the fulfilment of his divine duties, reflecting the transient yet significant impact of life's journeys. Hanuman, granted immortality, symbolizes ceaseless devotion, while Vibhishana's longevity rewards his righteousness, emphasizing the enduring value of virtues that guide subsequent generations.

These narratives highlight the timeless lessons of loyalty, duty, and the soul's immortality, offering profound insights into life's spiritual dimensions.

12.5 Meaning of the Hunter in 'Maa Nishada'

The hunter from Sage Valmiki's initial "Maa Nishada" sloka is ultimately revealed to be the divine trinity: Brahma, Vishnu, and Shiva. Rama, an incarnation of Vishnu, represents the sustaining power, while Brahma symbolizes creation and Shiva signifies destruction and regeneration. This trinity encapsulates the cosmic cycle of creation, preservation, and dissolution, serving as the hunter that causes the separation of illusion from ego and Maya, perpetuating a virtuous cycle of realization.

In the Ramayana, the worship of Shiva by both the hero, Rama, and the villain, Ravana, illustrates the nuanced interplay between devotion, ego, and divine intent. While both characters demonstrate reverence to Shiva, Ravana's downfall underscores the critical lesson that mere devotion without moral integrity is unsustainable. This highlights the essential role of righteousness underlying true spiritual practice, emphasizing that unchecked ego, despite religious devotion, inevitably leads to ruin.

The roles of Lava and Kusha, who continue the legacy by ruling after Rama, underscore the theme of regeneration and the perpetuation of dharma through progeny.

Thus, the hunter's identity as the divine trinity reinforces the ongoing evolution and cyclical nature of the universe, where creation, preservation, and destruction are in constant interplay, shaping the destiny of all beings. This revelation adds a profound layer to the Ramayana, highlighting the interconnectedness of all divine forces and the eternal journey of life and spirituality.

Certainly, the Ramayana stands as one of the greatest contributions of Vedic civilization to the world!

By now, one would have realized that the secret to unravelling the "facts" hidden in the "story" requires deciphering the characters in the story as attributes within every human being.

yaavat sthasyanti girayah saritah cha mahitale

taavat raamayana kathaa lokeshu pracharishyati

ch 2, Sarga 36, BalaKanda

"As long as mountains stand tall and rivers flow on Earth, the story of the Ramayana will spread throughout the world".

12.6 Mystery of Sita's Agnipariksha , Abandonment and Return to mother earth

The narrative of Sita's Agnipariksha, abandonment, and her eventual return to Earth in the Ramayana offers a compelling allegory for personal spiritual growth and moral resilience as interpreted below.

Why was Sita's Agnipariksha necessary?

Sita's Agnipariksha (trial by fire) was deemed necessary to prove her unwavering purity and virtue to the world after her time in Lanka, which was fraught with trials and exposure to material desires, symbolized by the golden deer that led to her abduction and confinement. This trial was not just about proving her spiritual and moral integrity, which had been called into question due to her prolonged exposure to Ravana's kingdom. The Agnipariksha symbolizes a critical moment where an individual must demonstrate their allegiance to spiritual growth over worldly distractions and the illusions created by the ego.

Self-reflective questions

- Reflecting on the symbolism of Sita's Agnipariksha in the Ramayana

  ○ How do you balance material desires with spiritual growth in your daily life?

  ○ How do you see your own spiritual resilience being tested in everyday life?

  ○ Consider the moments when you're faced with the allure of material desires or ego-driven decisions, How do you reconcile these challenges with your commitment to spiritual growth and integrity?

Why was Sita abandoned during her pregnancy?

Sita's abandonment during her pregnancy, spurred by societal scepticism about the purity of her unborn children, reflects the idea that individual karma, rather than lineage or heritage, influences one's life path, challenging the assumption that children automatically inherit the spiritual and moral stature of their parents. This emphasizes that each person must undertake their own spiritual and moral journey, underscoring the belief that there are no inherently superior races or lineages; personal evolution is determined solely by one's actions

Her children, Kusha and Lava, embody potential states of human existence—bliss (Kusha) and profound emotional love (Lava). Their governance, potentially extending the ethical and spiritual reign initiated by their father, Rama, suggests the possibility of a society thriving under continued righteous leadership, emphasizing the importance of moral integrity in leadership.

Self-reflective questions

- Reflecting on the allegory of Sita's Abandonment in the Ramayana

- In what ways do you think your background or heritage influences your life choices? How do you maintain independence in your moral and spiritual decisions?

- Considering the notion that each person's destiny is shaped by their own karma, how do you reconcile this with the idea of inherited traits or familial legacy?

- Considering the portrayal of Kusha and Lava, how do you think leadership should be influenced by moral and ethical integrity? Reflect on qualities you believe are essential for righteous leadership today.

Why did Sita decide to go back to mother earth and end her avatar, before Rama?

Sita's return to Mother Earth symbolizes the completion of her earthly roles and duties. Her departure before Rama underscores the transient yet impactful nature of avatars, who come to restore righteousness and depart after fulfilling their cosmic purposes. Sita's return is also a profound assertion of her autonomy and purity, choosing to leave the earthly realm on her own terms rather than continue to face unjust societal judgments. This act highlights the theme of personal sacrifice and liberation from worldly suffering, reinforcing her role as a moral and spiritual exemplar whose lessons transcend her physical presence.

Self-reflective questions

- Reflecting on the allegory of Sita's Return to Mother earth in the Ramayana,

- What do you consider your core responsibilities in life, and how do you know when they are fulfilled? How do you approach the idea of letting go once your role in a particular area is complete?

- In what ways have you made personal sacrifices for a greater good or higher purpose? How do you balance self-sacrifice with self-care and personal boundaries?

- How do you interpret the transient yet impactful nature of those who influence your life? Reflect on someone who has come into your life briefly but left a profound impact.

Chapter 13

The Rama Rajya Governance Lessons

Before delving into the concept of Rama Rajya, it is essential to understand the foundation upon which it was built. The kingdom of Ayodhya, under the rule of King Dasharatha, was already a well-established realm with a long history of prosperity, justice, and good governance. Ayodhya, one of the most ancient and revered cities in Bharat Varsha (ancient India), was renowned for its grandeur, cultural richness, and the harmonious life its citizens enjoyed.

The Reign of Dasharatha

Under Dasharatha's rule, Ayodhya was a flourishing kingdom, known for its adherence to dharma (righteousness). The king was respected not only for his valor but also for his wisdom and commitment to justice. The governance in Ayodhya was marked by fairness, compassion, and a deep sense of duty toward the welfare of its people. The citizens lived in peace, engaged in their respective duties, and enjoyed a quality of life that was both materially and spiritually fulfilling.

The kingdom was prosperous, with fertile lands, abundant resources, and thriving trade. The people were virtuous, law-abiding, and dedicated to their roles in society, whether as farmers, artisans, warriors, or scholars. The social fabric of Ayodhya was woven with the principles of dharma, and this created a strong, cohesive society where everyone's needs were met, and no one was left behind.

Ayodhya: A Kingdom Steeped in History: Ayodhya's legacy as a long-standing kingdom is significant. It was a city of great antiquity, steeped in traditions that had been passed down through generations. The city itself was an architectural marvel, with well-planned streets, majestic palaces, and temples that echoed the devotion of its people. Ayodhya was not just a political center but a cultural and spiritual hub where art, literature, and philosophy flourished.

Dasharatha's reign was characterized by a stable and just administration that upheld the values of dharma, ensuring that Ayodhya remained a beacon of prosperity and peace in Bharat Varsha. The king's decisions were guided by the counsel of wise ministers and sages, and his rule was marked by a deep concern for the well-being of his subjects.

Rama's Advice to Bharata

As Rama prepared to embark on his 14-year exile, he knew that the fate of Ayodhya would rest in the hands of his beloved brother, Bharata. This was no ordinary transfer of power; it was an opportunity for Rama to impart his profound understanding of what it truly meant to rule. The wisdom he shared with Bharata would not only guide the kingdom through his absence but would also become a timeless blueprint for righteous governance.

The Foundation of Dharma: Rama began by emphasizing the cornerstone of any just rule: dharma, or righteousness. He urged

Bharata to make dharma the guiding principle of his reign. "A king's actions," Rama explained, "must always align with the principles of justice, truth, and fairness. Place the welfare of the kingdom and its people above all personal interests." In these words, Rama encapsulated the essence of moral leadership, where the ruler is not driven by personal ambition but by the duty to uphold what is right and just.

A Guardian, Not Just a Ruler: Rama then turned to the concept of leadership itself. "Bharata," he said, "you must see yourself not just as a ruler, but as a guardian of the people. Their well-being should be your foremost concern." Rama's advice was a reminder that a king's true power lies in his ability to protect and care for his subjects. He encouraged Bharata to be accessible, to listen to the grievances of the people, and to act with compassion. "A king," Rama emphasized, "should be like a father to his subjects, providing for them and shielding them from harm."

The Wisdom of Counsel: Recognizing the complexities of governance, Rama advised Bharata on the importance of seeking counsel from the wise. "Surround yourself with ministers, sages, and scholars whose wisdom will guide you," he said. "Never act on impulse or personal bias; let your decisions be shaped by the collective knowledge of those you trust." For Rama, the strength of a ruler was not in solitary decision-making, but in the ability to draw from the wisdom of others. This advice underscored the value of humility and the recognition that true leadership is often a collaborative effort.

Law, Order, and Justice: Rama's counsel extended to the administration of justice, a pillar of any stable society. "Maintain strict law and order in the kingdom," he urged. "Do not allow corruption or injustice to take root. The laws of the land must be upheld, and justice must be administered fairly and swiftly." Rama knew that the prosperity and peace of Ayodhya depended on the rule of law. By emphasizing the importance of justice, he ensured that Bharata would govern a kingdom where order and fairness prevailed.

Promoting Prosperity and Welfare: A king's duty, according to Rama, went beyond maintaining law and order; it also involved fostering prosperity. "Support agriculture, trade, and industry," he advised. "Ensure that the people have the means to prosper and that the vulnerable are cared for." Rama's vision of governance was holistic, recognizing that the true measure of a king's success was the well-being of his people. By promoting economic growth and social welfare, Bharata would ensure that Ayodhya remained a land of abundance and contentment.

Respect for All Faiths: Rama, known for his deep respect for all forms of worship, encouraged Bharata to maintain this inclusivity. "Respect all religions and traditions," he said. "Foster a culture where all faiths are honored, and religious leaders are respected." In a kingdom as diverse as Ayodhya, Rama understood that unity could only be achieved through mutual respect and tolerance. This advice was a call to Bharata to rule with a spirit of inclusivity, ensuring harmony among the kingdom's diverse populations.

Ruling with Humility: Finally, Rama imparted a lesson on the character of a true leader. "Rule with humility," he counseled. "Remember that a king's power is not for personal glory but for the service of the people." Rama's advice was a reminder that the highest form of leadership is selfless service. He encouraged Bharata to be compassionate, to lead with a spirit of humility, and to recognize that his role as king was to serve, not to dominate.

A Legacy of Righteous Rule: As Bharata listened to Rama's counsel, he was deeply moved by the responsibility placed upon him. Despite his sorrow at being separated from his brother, Bharata accepted the role of regent with a profound sense of duty. In a symbolic act of devotion, he placed Rama's sandals on the throne, ruling in Rama's name until his return. This gesture reflected Bharata's commitment to upholding the principles that Rama had laid out, and it set the tone for a rule that would be marked by justice, compassion, and righteousness.

The Expansion of Rama Rajya: A Unified Bharat Varsha

After the epic events of the Ramayana, when Rama ascended the throne of Ayodhya, the concept of Rama Rajya began to take shape. Rama Rajya, often described as the ideal rule, was not limited to Ayodhya alone. Through Rama's victories in Lanka, Kishkindha, and other regions, this model of governance was extended to all the lands of Bharat Varsha.

Lanka, once under the tyrannical rule of Ravana, was transformed into a just and prosperous kingdom under Vibhishana's leadership, guided by the principles of Rama Rajya. Kishkindha, the land of the Vanaras, also came under this governance after the defeat of Vali and the establishment of Sugriva as the king. These lands, along with other territories in Bharat Varsha, were unified under a system of governance that was rooted in dharma, compassion, and justice.

Rama Rajya was characterized by the same virtues that had flourished during Dasharatha's reign, but with an even greater emphasis on the welfare of all beings, the upholding of righteousness, and the pursuit of spiritual and material prosperity. It was a time when the rulers were just, the people were virtuous, and the land was blessed with abundance and peace.

Reign of Rama and Sita

Rama and Sita ruled Ayodhya for an extraordinary period, traditionally said to be eleven thousand years, a symbolic representation of a timeless, perfect reign. During this time, they embodied the principles of dharma, setting an example of virtuous leadership that was deeply rooted in justice, compassion, and unwavering commitment to the well-being of their subjects.

Rama, as king, upheld the values he had advised Bharata on before his exile. His governance was characterized by fairness and impartiality, ensuring that justice was administered without prejudice. Rama was not just a ruler but a guardian of his people, deeply involved in the affairs of the kingdom, always accessible, and ever attentive to the needs of his subjects. He listened to their concerns, resolved disputes with wisdom, and maintained a society where the rule of law was respected by all.

Sita, as queen, played an equally vital role in the administration of Ayodhya. Her influence extended beyond the royal palace, as she embodied the ideals of compassion, virtue, and moral integrity. Sita was revered not only as the consort of Rama but as a symbol of purity and devotion, a figure who inspired the women of Ayodhya to lead lives of dignity and grace. Her presence in the royal court brought balance and harmony, complementing Rama's rule with her wisdom and insight.

The Emotional State of the Subjects: Under the rule of Rama and Sita, the people of Ayodhya experienced an emotional state of unparalleled contentment and security. There was a deep sense of connection between the rulers and the ruled, a bond forged by mutual respect and affection. The subjects of Ayodhya viewed Rama and Sita not merely as sovereigns, but as divine embodiments of righteousness and love. This relationship fostered a sense of loyalty and devotion that permeated the entire kingdom.

The emotional well-being of the people was further enhanced by the stability and fairness of the governance they experienced. There were no grievances left unaddressed, no injustices that went uncorrected. The subjects lived without fear of tyranny, knowing that their king and queen were guided by dharma in every decision they made. This assurance brought a sense of peace and fulfillment to their lives, allowing them to thrive in all aspects—socially, economically, and spiritually.

The Quality of Life in Ayodhya: The quality of life during the reign of Rama and Sita was nothing short of idyllic. Ayodhya became a model of prosperity and harmony, where every citizen enjoyed the fruits of good governance. The economy flourished under Rama's leadership; agriculture, trade, and industry thrived, leading to an abundance of resources that were equitably distributed among the people. Poverty and hunger were virtually nonexistent, as Rama ensured that even the most vulnerable in society were cared for. The streets of Ayodhya were clean and well-maintained, the markets bustling with activity, and the temples filled with devotees offering prayers in an atmosphere of spiritual serenity. Education and the arts were highly valued, with schools and cultural institutions receiving royal patronage. Festivals and communal gatherings were frequent, fostering a strong sense of community and shared identity among the people.

Law and order were impeccably maintained, with Rama's administration ensuring that justice was swift and fair. There was no crime, no deceit, and no corruption, as the principles of dharma were deeply ingrained in the fabric of society. The people were virtuous, their lives guided by moral values that reflected the teachings of their king and queen.

Leadership qualities to bring about Rama Rajya

A leader in the ideal of Rama Rajya must embody selfless service. The leader's role is not to seek personal gain or power but to serve the people with humility. This quality ensures that decisions are made with the well-being of the people in mind, rather than the leader's own interests. Humility allows the leader to stay grounded, acknowledging that the true strength of a kingdom lies in the happiness and welfare of its subjects.

Adherence to Dharma: Dharma, or righteousness, is the cornerstone of effective leadership in Rama Rajya. A leader must always act in accordance with Dharma, ensuring that justice and fairness guide every action. This adherence to Dharma maintains the moral integrity of the kingdom and fosters trust among the people. By prioritizing righteousness over personal desires, the leader ensures that the kingdom remains in harmony and that the principles of justice and truth are upheld.

Compassion and Justice: Compassion is another critical quality for a leader within Rama Rajya. A ruler must treat all subjects with kindness and understanding, acting as a guardian who protects and nurtures the well-being of the people. Alongside compassion, a strong sense of justice is essential. The leader must ensure that fairness prevails in the kingdom, with laws applied equally to all, regardless of status or power. This balance of compassion and justice helps to create a society where people feel secure and valued.

Commitment to the Greater Good: A leader's focus must always be on the greater good, putting the needs of the kingdom above personal desires or family ties. As demonstrated by Rama, even when faced with difficult decisions, the leader must prioritize the long-term welfare of the people and the kingdom. This commitment to the greater good ensures that the leader's actions contribute to the prosperity and stability of the realm, even if it requires personal sacrifice.

Symbolic Leadership and Legacy: Rama's decision to entrust Bharata with the kingdom, symbolized by placing his sandals on the throne, underscores the importance of symbolic leadership. The leader must be a living embodiment of the kingdom's values and principles, serving as a role model for others to follow. This symbolic leadership helps to reinforce the ideals of Rama Rajya and ensures that these principles are passed down through generations, creating a lasting legacy of righteousness and good governance.

These qualities—selfless service, adherence to Dharma, compassion, justice, commitment to the greater good, and symbolic leadership—are essential for any leader aspiring to establish and maintain Rama Rajya, the ideal kingdom of peace, prosperity, and righteousness.

The Legacy of Rama Rajya

The reign of Rama and Sita left an indelible mark on the history of Ayodhya and Bharat Varsha as a whole. It was a period when the ideals of dharma were not just preached but practiced at every level of society. The concept of Rama Rajya became synonymous with a utopian vision of governance—one where justice, compassion, and prosperity were accessible to all.

Rama's rule, supported by Sita's wisdom and virtue, created a legacy that transcended time, becoming the benchmark for all subsequent rulers who sought to govern justly. The golden age of their reign continues to inspire leaders and citizens alike, serving as a reminder of what is possible when governance is guided by the highest principles of righteousness.

The emotional state of the subjects and the quality of life they enjoyed during this era were testaments to the effectiveness of Rama's model of governance. It was a time when the kingdom was not just a political entity but a reflection of the divine order, where every individual, regardless of status, found their rightful place in a society dedicated to the collective good.

Rama Rajya symbolizes an ideal state of harmony within the individual psyche. In our inner spiritual kingdom, Ayodhya, we rule with compassion, justice, kindness, and love, leading to a deep sense of contentment. Under Rama Rajya in our inner Lanka, we conquer arrogance, pride, and the illusion of invincibility, replacing them with self-restraint, humility, and inner peace. This fosters a life free from the tyranny of material desires and the ego. In the inner kingdom of Kishkindha, devotion and mutual respect guide our instincts, ensuring balance and contentment. Rama Rajya is not just a societal vision; it is a personal journey of spiritual alignment, where justice, compassion, and self-restraint govern our inner world.

In a Nutshell

The " Ramayana Secrets" explores into a spiritual battle within each person, where overcoming ego and material desires—symbolized by Lanka—is essential. This internal conflict is resolved by aligning the mind with divine virtues, as exemplified by the inhabitants of Kishkindha and Ayodhya, and achieving mastery over the senses, illustrated by Vibhishana's governance in Lanka.

The narrative also suggests that each generation must undertake its own spiritual journey, reflecting the ongoing themes of the Ramayana through the lives of Rama's descendants, Lava and Kusha. Sita's abandonment highlights the unpredictability of spiritual inheritance, emphasizing that spiritual qualities are shaped by individual karma rather than guaranteed by ancestral purity or divinity.

At its core, the notion of Rama Rajya should represent not just an idealized form of governance, but a state of internal harmony where dharma guides every aspect of life, ensuring justice, compassion, and self-realization for all.

If the Ramayana is not a literal historical narrative, how can one explain the existence of so many physical places that correlate with the epic?

Answer:

The Ramayana unfolds not only as an external narrative but as an allegory of the inner spiritual journey in addition. The physical places mentioned in the epic, such as Ayodhya, Lanka, and Kishkindha, correlate with human experiences across time. Human beings indeed existed in these regions, and the events of the Ramayana happened as representations of deeper spiritual truths. However, the subtle qualities and inner traits personified by the characters and events—such as ego (Ravana), devotion (Hanuman), and virtue (Rama)— exist within the psyche of every individual in those places.

When examining these sites archaeologically, no remains can directly prove or disprove the existence of the individuals described in the Ramayana because the traits they represent reside within human consciousness. Proving the historicity of the epic through physical evidence, while fascinating, may not fully grasp the abstract, allegorical layer of the narrative. The epic exists in both the tangible and intangible realms, with its true significance lying beyond physical artifacts, in the spiritual lessons it offers.

Archaeology

The challenge of uncovering physical evidence for characters from epics like the Ramayana and Mahabharata through archaeology is rooted in the nature of the texts themselves. These epics are primarily spiritual and moral allegories as well as depicting historical facts. Depictions of divinities such as Rama, Krishna, Sita, and Hanuman go beyond historical figures; they symbolize universal human qualities—divinity, devotion, greed, and ego. These qualities are abstract, existing within the psychological and spiritual realms, representing the core traits of human nature and experience, rather than physical entities that could be uncovered through archaeological means.

Their significance lies in the moral and ethical challenges they embody, transcending the need for physical evidence. While these characters may not leave behind tangible artifacts, they embody qualities that are very much alive within the human experience, resonating deeply in the collective consciousness. These traits, though unseen, are pervasive across humanity, making the impact of these characters felt in every individual.

Is the Ramayana true? Yes, it's true for every human being who has experienced this journey of inner evolution since Treta Yuga!

This perspective highlights the profound understanding of human nature by ancient sages like Valmiki. They crafted these stories to reflect eternal truths about the human condition, making them timeless and universally relevant. The events and characters, while narrated vividly, symbolize the internal battles each person faces, making the Ramayana 'true' not in a historical sense, but in a psychological and spiritual sense—depicting universal truths that transcend time.

Western scholarship often seeks physical evidence to validate historical claims, but this approach can misunderstand the intent of the *itihasas*. These texts weren't meant as literal historical accounts but as vehicles to communicate deeper truths. The focus on physical evidence overlooks the true purpose of these epics: to explore life's spiritual and moral complexities. While they have a historical context, their real value lies in their ability to guide us through life's inner challenges.

While archaeological discoveries may shed light on ancient civilizations, they are unlikely to reveal the deeper, metaphorical meanings within the *itihasas*. These stories remain profoundly important and true in their depiction of the human journey and the eternal struggle within our nature.

Interpreting these epics as class struggles, as some leftist perspectives do, imposes a foreign framework that misses the point. Such views overlook the epics' focus on spiritual evolution and ethical dilemmas, which differ greatly from Marxist analyses centred on economic and power dynamics. The *itihasas* emphasize divine oneness and unity in diversity, highlighting the interconnectedness of all existence.

Pilgrimage and Piety through Ramayana's Sacred Journeys

Having explored "Ramayana Secrets" at an abstract level, it does reveal that temple worship and pilgrimages to locations linked to the Ramayana are not merely physical acts of devotion but are deeply symbolic of the inner spiritual journey. These sacred practices serve as catalysts for personal growth, embodying the virtues depicted in the epic.

Temples and pilgrimage sites connected to the Ramayana provide a tangible link to its profound teachings. The lore of these places, known as "sthala puranas," enhances their spiritual significance, making pilgrimages journeys of self-discovery and purification.

Engaging in these rituals and visiting sacred sites helps externalize internal spiritual quests, providing a break from daily routines and fostering reflection on life paths and divine qualities such as righteousness and selflessness.

In contemporary life, where stress and disconnection are common, these age-old practices offer grounding and continuity with historical values, aiding in handling modern challenges. They reinforce lessons from the Ramayana like duty and integrity, guiding ethical choices and deeper life purposes.

Thus, these temples and pilgrimages affirm the ongoing relevance of the Ramayana's teachings in navigating modern existence, symbolizing the personal and societal journey toward spiritual and moral enlightenment.

Epilogue

PART A - Revisiting Specific Criticisms of Lord Rama

This epilogue explores the diverse criticisms levelled at the Ramayana, delving into their origins and the epic's inherently expansive and exploratory nature. Such criticisms often arise from the Ramayana's capacity for open-ended interpretation and its profound integration into diverse cultural, spiritual, and philosophical dialogues. With its complex layers of moral and ethical dilemmas, the Ramayana encourages a wide range of interpretations and analyses, leading to varied perspectives on its characters and narratives.

The epilogue also seeks to demonstrate why these debates are not only inevitable but crucial for maintaining the epic's relevance and dynamism in modern discussions. It emphasizes that the exploratory layer of abstraction presented in "Ramayana Secrets" helps to enrich these discussions, offering new ways of understanding the epic's enduring appeal and significance.

Rama's Decision to Honor Kaikeyi's Order and Go into Exile (Ayodhya Kanda, Chapter 19)

Criticism: This decision reflects rigid adherence to duty at the expense of personal welfare.

Interpretation: Rama's exile is an allegory for the loss of divine innocence as a child, navigating the complexities of growing up. Just as Rama's departure leads him into the wilderness, growing up embarks individuals on a metaphorical journey through life's wilderness to reclaim their divine nature and is proven in hindsight.

Treatment of Shurpanakha, Resulting in Her Disfigurement (Aranya Kanda, Chapter 19)

Criticism: The harsh treatment of Shurpanakha, who expresses her desire for Rama, is often seen as excessive.

Interpretation: Shurpanakha symbolizes temptations and covetous desires for material possessions or inappropriate relationships. Her advances and rejection signify the importance of resisting such temptations and maintaining integrity. Disfiguring her represents the decisive rejection of unethical or harmful desires, highlighting the need to take a firm stand against them.

Killing of Vali While in Hiding (Kishkindha Kanda, Chapter 16)

Criticism: Rama's act of killing Vali from behind a tree during his fight with Sugreeva is often criticized for being against the principles of fair combat.

Interpretation: Vali represents the instinctive mind—powerful but often driven by impulses that conflict with higher spiritual goals. His formidable strength leads to behaviour detrimental to ethical and spiritual growth. Rama's concealed approach to kill Vali symbolizes the essential subduing of these lower instincts to elevate divine consciousness. This act suggests that as spiritual awareness heightens, instinctive and primal forces get controlled to achieve higher moral and spiritual aims. Rama's concealment during the killing of Vali symbolizes that such transformations are both inevitable and necessary.

Rama's Handling of Ravana, Requiring Divine Support (Yuddha Kanda)

Criticism: Rama's reliance on divine support, requiring Indras chariot and Sage Agastya's weapons and mantra, rather than confronting Ravana directly has been critiqued.

Interpretation: Spiritually, it highlights the importance of divine support and acknowledging a higher power in overcoming significant adversities, even for a manifested avatar.

Testing Sita's Purity Through Agni Pareeksha (Yuddha Kanda, Chapter 118)

Criticism: This trial is seen as a reflection of mistrust and insensitivity.

Interpretation: Rama's request for Sita to undergo Agni Pareeksha was not due to personal doubt but to ensure that the people of Ayodhya and the entire world recognized her purity. His request for her to dress in her finest attire underscores his respect and love for her, desiring her to be seen as the noble queen she was. The divine intervention by Agni and Indra highlights cosmic justice that endorses Sita's virtue, leaving no doubt of her honour and elevating the moral victory of Rama and Sita.

Exile of Sita During Her Pregnancy (Uttara Kanda, Chapters 42-43)

Criticism: Critics argue that Rama's decision reflects a blind adherence to societal expectations over personal trust and justice.

Interpretation: The doubts arise during Sita's pregnancy, emphasizing the societal questions regarding the purity and worthiness of their future offspring. This is society doubting the purity and worthiness of future offspring....a question that has no answer. One cannot have any faith on that, the next generation too must go through their own transformative journeys. The children, like Lava and Kusha, must evolve independently, highlighting their continuous cycle of personal transformation. This is no doubt the most intriguing part of the Ramayana.

Abandoning Lakshman Due to a Breach of Promise (Uttara Kanda, Chapter 94)

Criticism: This act is often viewed as extreme adherence to principles over familial bonds.

Interpretation: As one approaches the end of life, the need for focus and vigilance wanes. Upon death, these qualities also fade. However, the power of devotion, represented by Hanuman, is eternal and transcends into the next life.

In the epic, soon after Lakshman's departure, Rama also leaves. This transformative journey reappears in cycles, illustrating that human beings must continually evolve to a higher-level generation after generation.

Why did Ravana refrain from molesting Sita despite his lustful nature as depicted in the Valmiki Ramayana?

A: Ravana's restraint towards Sita, despite his lustful nature, can be attributed to multiple factors. First, he was cursed by Rambha, a celestial nymph, who warned that if he ever forced himself upon an unwilling woman, his head would shatter into pieces. This curse instilled a fear in him that stopped him from harming Sita.

Secondly, Sita's divine purity and unwavering devotion to Rama created a protective aura around her. Ravana, despite his arrogance, couldn't bring himself to violate her virtue. His ego also played a key role—he wanted Sita to willingly submit to him as a way of proving his superiority over Rama. He believed that through manipulation and time, he could win her over. Lastly, Ravana's restraint can also be seen as part of the larger cosmic plan, ensuring the epic journey towards his eventual downfall unfolds as destined.

Together, these factors prevented Ravana from acting on his lustful impulses, making his treatment of Sita a crucial part of the Ramayana's narrative.

PART B – Summary of the key interpretations in "Ramayana Secrets"

This book interprets the Ramayana by viewing its characters as personifications of internal traits rather than historical figures, encouraging readers to see these characters as aspects of their own psyche.

Rama's journey is presented as a metaphor for personal growth, where one strives to achieve a state akin to Rama Rajya, where the divine self-reigns over ego and sensory desires. The alignment of the Vanaras, symbolizing the human mind, with figures like Hanuman (devotion) and Sugriva (emotion) is central to this process.

This framework offers insights into our nature and internal battles, guiding readers toward self-realization and mastery over their inner world. A summary follows.

Why is Kaikeyi the favourite wife of King Dasharatha?

Kaikeyi is often depicted as King Dasharatha's favourite wife due to her profound qualities of determination and resilience, which play a significant symbolic role in the narrative of the Ramayana. Dasharatha, representing the human body and psyche governed by the ten "faculties"- five Jnana Indriyas (cognitive faculties) and five Karma Indriyas (action faculties) (see 5.1) - finds a unique alignment with Kaikeyi's characteristics. In the epic, she is portrayed as having the willpower and courage to support and maintain the functionality of these 'indriyas', metaphorically illustrated through her actions during a battle where she manages the chariot and aids an injured Dasharatha.

Her ability to keep the chariot, symbolic of the body and senses, moving even when damaged, and her skill in healing Dasharatha highlight her as an essential stabilizing force. This capability symbolizes her role in keeping the human being's sense faculty and actions aligned and operational, which can also manifest as stubbornness—a trait that leads to significant plot developments such as Rama's exile. This aspect of her character underscores the complex interplay of virtues and flaws within a person, portraying her not just as a support system but also as an agent of pivotal change within the narrative. (for more detailed explanations read sec 5.1)

What do Kausalya, Sumitra personify as also the divine children of King Dasharatha?

Kausalya, the mother of Rama, personifies the good and beneficial vibrations inherent in the faculties (indriyas). She represents the nurturing and righteous aspect that fosters the ideal qualities in Rama, who is seen as the embodiment of virtue and the ideal hero.

Sumitra, mother of twins Lakshman and Shatrughna, represents inherent amicability and supportiveness. Lakshman, closely associated with Rama, symbolizes focus and dedication, often acting as Rama's unwavering companion and protector.

Shatrughna, who plays a less prominent role in the epic, mirrors the traits of harmony and service, underlined by his commitment to family and dharma.

Bharata, son of Kaikeyi, embodies the capacity to bear burdens and uphold responsibilities, traits he inherits from his mother's strong will and determination. Despite the controversial circumstances brought about by Kaikeyi which led to Rama's exile, Bharata demonstrates profound integrity by refusing to take the throne and instead rules Ayodhya as Rama's regent, symbolizing loyalty and righteousness.

Each of these characters not only contributes to the narrative of the Ramayana but also offers insights into the values and virtues upheld in the epic, highlighting the interplay of duty, righteousness, and familial bonds.

What do Sita personify and meaning of her birth in a furrow?

Sita embodies the intrinsic power of faith and goodness, perfectly complementing Rama's virtues. Her role extends beyond that of a wife; she symbolizes the inner strength and moral integrity that Rama, as the ideal of Dharma, seeks to uphold. Sita represents the unwavering faith and virtue that support and elevate the principles of Dharma in Rama's journey.

Sita's birth from a furrow symbolizes the deep-rooted and intrinsic nature of all beings to stay aligned with virtues and goodness. This inherent alignment to moral principles is a fundamental aspect of one's existence. It is this inner faith, grounded in virtue, that guides and drives all actions, serving as a steadfast moral compass throughout life."

Ravana's desire to possess Sita represents his alignment and attachment to adharma (unrighteousness), showcasing the unsustainable nature of such desires and setting the stage for the epic narrative of the Ramayana. Sita's abduction and her time in Lanka metaphorically reflect the trials possibly most human beings undergo—captured by ego and sensory allurements.

The journey to rescue Sita is emblematic of the quest to reclaim one's inner faith and align it back with goodness and spiritual path that every individual is destined to navigate.

This interpretation of Sita's story as central to the Ramayana's theme explains why the epic is sometimes referred to as the "Sitayana," emphasizing her pivotal role in the unfolding of events that lead to the triumph of dharma over adharma.

What do the kingdoms of Ayodhya, Kishkindha and Lanka represent?

The kingdoms of Ayodhya, Kishkindha, and Lanka in the Ramayana represent different aspects of the inner world within every human being, each symbolizing a unique dimension of our consciousness and life experiences.

Ayodhya: Ayodhya represents the inner kingdom of the "indriyas" (senses and faculties) (see sec 5.1) In Ayodhya, rulers and princes govern life in a morally and spiritually appropriate manner. It symbolizes a state of inner governance where the principles of dharma (righteousness) are upheld, ensuring harmony and balance within oneself. When Rama rules Ayodhya, it becomes an epitome of Rama Rajya, a just and orderly rule based on the principles of dharma. This reflects an ideal state of being where the mind and senses are aligned with moral values, leading to a life of peace and fulfilment.

Lanka: Lanka, on the other hand, represents an inner kingdom dominated by the senses and egoistic pursuits. It is a realm where the pursuit of wealth, power, and hedonistic pleasures takes precedence, often at the cost of disregarding true divine nature and engaging in actions that border on adharma (unrighteousness). While the inhabitants of this inner kingdom may be talented and capable, their actions are driven by ego and desire, leading to a disconnect from spiritual truth and righteousness.

Kishkindha: symbolizes the kingdom of the Vanaras (monkey-like beings), representing the different facets of the mind, which are often dominated by restless, monkey-like thoughts. This kingdom is governed by the instinctive mind (represented by Vali) and the emotional mind (represented by Sugriva), with the devotional mind (symbolized by Hanuman) playing a crucial supportive role. Kishkindha's alignment with Rama in the quest to redeem Sita, who represents faith, is vital as it enables the inner faculties to overcome the egoistic and sensory illusions—referred to in Vedic philosophy as Maya. Essentially the restless mind when aligned with higher principles transcend illusions created by the senses and ego.

Who are the principal characters of Lanka and what do they personify?

A short summary of some key personifications:

Ravana: Ravana is the king of Lanka, symbolizing the egoistic, hedonistic ruler within us. He personifies the unchecked ego that seeks power, pleasure, and self-indulgence at any cost. Ravana was considered invincible until the events of the Ramayana, which illustrate the power within human beings to subdue this powerful force of ego through the alignment with higher virtues and principles.

Indrajit: Indrajit, Ravana's son and the next most powerful figure in Lanka, represents the sense of invincibility and pride that often leads to illusory thinking. He embodies the arrogance that comes from power and the belief in one's invulnerability, which blinds individuals to the consequences of their actions.

Kumbhakarna: Kumbhakarna, Ravana's brother, personifies the power pangs of hunger and the unending need for sensory gratification. His immense size and insatiable appetite symbolize the overwhelming desires and addictions that can consume a person, leading them to neglect higher spiritual aspirations in favour of momentary pleasures.

Surpanakha: Surpanakha, Ravana's sister, represents the urge to be covetous and the insatiable desire to possess what is not rightfully one's own. Her character embodies the destructive nature of envy and unbridled desire, which can lead to chaos and suffering.

Vibhishana: Vibhishana, Ravana's brother, stands in contrast to the other inhabitants of Lanka. He represents self-restraint, caution, and the inner voice of conscience that recognizes the difference between right and wrong. Vibhishana ultimately becomes the king of Lanka after Ravana's downfall and brings the kingdom under Rama Rajya—a rule guided by the principles of dharma and righteousness.

In summary, Lanka is a realm where various negative and destructive forces dominate, driven by ego, desire, and illusion. However, the presence of Vibhishana symbolizes the potential for redemption and the possibility of restoring balance through self-restraint and adherence to dharma. The characters of Lanka reflect the inner battles that individuals face in overcoming these lower tendencies and aligning themselves with higher spiritual values.

How did the Pushpaka Vimana function equally well for both Ravana and Rama?

The Pushpaka Vimana is not just a physical vehicle; it can be understood as a thought machine, a powerful enabler of thoughts, ambitions, and desires, controlled by the one who commands it. It functions as a divine vehicle that aligns with the intentions and will of its controller, amplifying their desires and ambitions, whether they are righteous or otherwise

When Ravana, driven by his egoistic and hedonistic desires, commanded the Pushpaka Vimana, it became an instrument of his ambitions. The Vimana participated in the abduction of Sita, a symbolic act of Ravana's attempt to possess what was not rightfully his. Furthermore, it was used to increase Sita's despair by showing her a false vision of the death of Rama and Lakshman, manipulating her emotions to further Ravana's intentions.

However, the same Pushpaka Vimana, when commanded by Rama, a paragon of dharma and righteousness, served a noble purpose. It hastened the return of Rama, Sita, and others to Ayodhya, symbolizing the Vimana's ability to align with and support virtuous intentions. The Pushpaka Vimana, therefore, can be seen as a divine vehicle that helps the ambition of its driver to flower and blossom, regardless of the nature of those ambitions.

A fitting name for this thought machine could be "Manoratha," reflecting its nature as a chariot of the mind, driven by the thoughts and desires of its controller. Whether it serves the cause of dharma or adharma depends on the intentions of the one who commands it, making it a powerful symbol of how tools and resources can be used for both good and bad, depending on the character and purpose of their wielder. (see also 9.3)

In the Valmiki Ramayana, Hanuman and the Vanaras use tree trunks and boulders instead of conventional weapons—what do symbolic weapons like bows, arrows, maces, and chariots represent?

Indeed, in the Valmiki Ramayana, Hanuman and the Vanaras do not wield conventional weapons like maces, swords, or bows and arrows. Instead, they engage in direct combat, using tree trunks, boulders, and their physical strength. This choice of "weapons" is deeply symbolic, reflecting the nature of the Vanaras and the inner battle that the epic represents.

The Vanaras, as embodiments of the mind and its various facets, uproot entrenched belief systems and use their sheer force to clobber sense into their adversaries. The act of uprooting trees and hurling boulders symbolizes the mind's power to dismantle old, rigid thought patterns and to counteract the attacks of the senses and ego.

Even Hanuman, who is often depicted with a mace in later versions and interpretations of the Ramayana, does not actually carry one in the Valmiki Ramayana. This absence is significant—it highlights that the true "weapons" in this inner war are not physical but symbolic. The Vanaras' tails are particularly important, as they help maintain balance and prevent them from being toppled. The tail, therefore, symbolizes the grounding of the mind, keeping it rooted and stable amidst the turmoil of inner conflict. In this sense, the tail becomes a vital weapon, ensuring that the mind remains balanced and does not lose its footing in the battle against the ego and sensory temptations.

As for the more conventional weapons seen in the epic, such as bows and arrows, maces, and chariots, they too have symbolic meanings:

Arrows: Arrows represent focused thoughts, precise and directed towards a specific target or goal. In the context of an inner war, they symbolize the power of concentrated intention and sharp mental focus that can pierce through the illusions and deceptions of the ego and senses.

Bows: Bows, as the launch vehicles for arrows, symbolize the mechanisms or faculties that direct and propel focused thoughts. They represent the willpower, intention, and inner resolve needed to aim and release thoughts towards achieving one's spiritual objectives.

Maces: Maces symbolize brute strength and the ability to crush obstacles. When present, they represent the mind's capacity to demolish gross negativities and overcome intense challenges through sheer force of will and determination.

Chariots: Chariots symbolize the body or vehicle of the soul that carries one through life's journey. They represent the controlled movement of the self, guided by the mind (the charioteer), towards higher spiritual goals.

Since the Ramayana is fundamentally a story of inner struggle and self-realization, these weapons need not be physical objects of metal or wood. Instead, they operate on a subtle level, symbolizing the mental and spiritual tools employed in the battle against the lower self.

This approach is characteristic of Itihasas (epic histories) like the Ramayana, which blend the physical with the metaphorical to convey deeper truths about the human condition and the journey toward enlightenment.

How do you reconcile the symbolic interpretations presented in this book with Valmiki's historical narrative and real locations, while honouring his storytelling to include fantastical elements like talking monkeys, flying machines, and magical weapons?

The symbolic interpretations in Ramayana Secrets strengthen the historicity of the epic, suggesting it reflects a significant period in human evolution, around 12,000 BC, when human consciousness advanced through the Rama avatar to conquer ego and sensory allurements. During this time, the mind, symbolized by the Vanaras, aligned with a higher purpose, enabling humanity to perceive and embody inner divinity.

Thus, the Ramayana is not merely a past event but a continuous process unfolding in the daily lives of individuals.

The true historical evidence of the Ramayana lies not in physical artifacts but in the intangible attributes of human consciousness—qualities such as kindness, compassion, moral orientation, devotion, and even negative traits like pride, envy, and anger—none of which can be discerned from physical remains alone. This is why archaeology may not uncover its remnants. While skeletal remains might testify to the existence of beings from that era, they cannot reveal the inner qualities and moral struggles that are central to the Ramayana's narrative

However, temples and pilgrimage sites linked to the Ramayana across India, Sri Lanka, and other regions influenced by Hindu civilization offer tangible connections to its teachings. Enriched by their "sthala puranas," these sites hold deep spiritual significance, making pilgrimages journeys of self-discovery and purification, and affirming the ongoing relevance of the Ramayana in every human life.

Thus, the symbolic interpretation is consistent with the epic's historicity, even addressing many of the "unbelievable" aspects of the storytelling. Additionally, elements of archeoastronomy further reinforce the historical grounding of the Ramayana, with the symbolic layer adding depth and strengthening its historical significance.

Summary of the "Ancient Facts" (Purva Yuktham) highlighted in "Ramayana Secrets"

"Ramayana Secrets" delves into the profound ancient truths surrounding the Rama avatar, believed to have taken place during the Treta Yuga, around 12,000 BC, as posited by researcher Nilesh Oak using archeoastronomy techniques. This era marked a significant elevation in human consciousness, largely attributed to the divine presence of Lord Rama, who appears as a mortal avatar within the consciousness of human beings.

His incarnation empowered individuals to transcend their ego and profane tendencies, symbolized by Ravana and Lanka, to achieve a higher state of spiritual awareness, moral integrity, and self-evolution.

The Vanaras (forest-dwelling monkey warriors) in the epic epitomize the untamed mind, which, through divine guidance, can be harnessed and directed toward spiritual transformation.

With the establishment of Rama's progeny as rulers, a virtuous cycle of self-purification and self-perpetuation began. This ongoing cycle is sustained by key human traits embodied by pivotal characters: self-restraint, as represented by Vibhishan, and unwavering devotion, exemplified by Hanuman. These virtues ensure the cycle's continuation, fostering human evolution through adherence to spiritual practices and maintaining faith in the divine.

The Ramayana also foresees the next evolutionary leap in human consciousness through the Krishna avatar with the establishment of Mathura by Rama's brother Shatrughna. In this phase, divisive thinking (Kamsa) is anticipated to be eradicated, and the potential of love (Krishna, Radha) will permeate human consciousness with the arrival of Krishna and his flute.

This evolution sets the stage for the eventual manifestation of the Kalki avatar, which remains yet to be revealed. The Kalki avatar is prophesied to further advance human evolution, marking another significant shift in the spiritual and moral consciousness of humanity.

"Ramayana Secrets" highlights this cyclical process of human and spiritual development. The progression from Rama to Krishna, and eventually to Kalki, underscores a continual journey toward higher consciousness and moral integrity. This journey is marked by the self-restraint of the ego and sensory urges, the fostering of love, and the ultimate unification of humanity under divine guidance. The timeless teachings of these avatars guide us to align our moral compass and embrace the eternal values that elevate human existence. As the Ramayana beautifully encapsulates, ***"In the quest for righteousness, the true victory lies in conquering one's inner demons and nurturing the divine within."***

Appendix I

The Many Ramayanas

The various versions of the Ramayana underscore its profound cultural and spiritual impact across regions and epochs. This appendix offers a detailed look at the diverse interpretations of the Ramayana, from Valmiki's foundational text to adaptations like Tulsidas's Ramcharitmanas and Kambar's Kamba Ramayanam, alongside feminist and non-Hindu versions such as the Jain Paumachariyam and the Malaysian Hikayat Seri Rama.

In the Jain rendition, Ravana emerges as a tragic hero, a stark contrast to his typical depiction as a villain. Camille Bulcke's Christian-influenced Ramkatha emphasizes ethical dimensions, paralleling Christian morals while focusing on Rama's human traits, thus sidelining his divine aspects. Meanwhile, the Hikayat Seri Rama adapts the story with local myths and Islamic influences, reshaping characters and plots to suit its cultural backdrop.

These adaptations demonstrate how the Ramayana has been tailored to meet the varying spiritual, ethical, and cultural needs of diverse communities, showcasing the epic's dynamic evolution over time. While the Valmiki Ramayana remains the Pramana (authoritative source), these varied interpretations enrich our understanding of its legacy and affirm its continuing relevance worldwide.

Here are 15 diverse and sometimes contentious variation for the readers to explore more, this appendix underscores the need for a deeper understanding of the Ramayana's enduring legacy and its dynamic evolution through history.

15 Important Ramayana Concepts and their Variations

Divinity of Rama:

- Valmiki: Rama is depicted as an incarnation of Vishnu, embodying divine attributes while also experiencing human emotions and struggles.

- Bulcke's Missionary lens: Emphasizes Rama's human qualities and moral character, potentially underplaying his divine aspects to highlight ethical lessons.

- Jain Approach: Views Rama as a virtuous human being rather than a divine entity.

- Leftist Approach: Often sceptical of the divine portrayal, seeing Rama more as a historical or mythological figure whose divinity is used to justify existing power structures and uphold Brahmanical supremacy.

- Malay Muslim Approach: Adapts Rama's divinity to fit local myths and Islamic influences.

Sita's Purity:

- Valmiki: Sita's purity and devotion are unquestioned, and her trial by fire (Agni Pariksha) reaffirms her chastity.

- Bulcke's Missionary lens: Focus on Sita's trial as a moral and ethical dilemma, interpreting it through a lens of personal integrity and suffering, akin to Christian martyrdom.

- Jain Approach: Focuses on Sita's virtue and inner strength.

- Leftist Approach: Criticizes the Agni Pariksha as patriarchal oppression, highlighting Sita's suffering as indicative of the broader systemic mistreatment of women.

- Malay Muslim Approach: May reinterpret Sita's trials in the context of Islamic values.

Concept of Dharma:

- Valmiki: Dharma (righteousness) is a complex and multifaceted concept central to the Ramayana, encompassing duty, justice, and moral order.

- Bulcke's Missionary lens: Interprets dharma more in line with Christian ethical principles, and simplify its nuances to fit a more universal moral framework.

- Jain Approach: Interprets dharma through the lens of Jain ethics and non-violence.

- Leftist Approach: Questions the traditional interpretation of dharma as reinforcing caste hierarchies and social inequalities, advocating for a more egalitarian understanding of justice.

- Malay Muslim Approach: Integrates Islamic concepts of righteousness and justice.

Role of Hanuman:

- Valmiki: Hanuman is a devoted servant of Rama, a symbol of selfless devotion and divine intervention.

- Bulcke's Missionary lens: Highlights Hanuman's role as a moral exemplar, highlighting his virtues in a way that parallels Christian saints and their devotion.

- Jain Approach: May downplay Hanuman's divine aspects, focusing on his moral actions.

- Leftist Approach: Sees Hanuman's unquestioning loyalty as a critique of servility and blind obedience, emphasizing the need for critical thinking and resistance against authoritarianism.

- Malay Muslim Approach: Reinterprets Hanuman within local folklore.

Ravana's Character:

- Valmiki: Ravana is portrayed as a complex antagonist with both admirable qualities and fatal flaws.

- Bulcke's Missionary lens: Interprets Ravana more straightforwardly as a symbol of evil, aligning with the Christian dichotomy of good versus evil.

- Jain Approach: Portrays Ravana as a tragic hero and scholar.

- Leftist Approach: Often reinterprets Ravana as a revolutionary figure challenging Brahmanical authority, highlighting his scholarly attributes and questioning the demonization of non-Aryan figures.

- Malay Muslim Approach: Ravana's role is adapted to fit local mythological contexts.

Concept of Sin and Redemption:

- Valmiki: The idea of sin in the Ramayana is tied to adharmic actions and the cosmic order rather than personal guilt and redemption.

- Bulcke's Missionary lens: Introduce concepts of sin and personal redemption in line with Christian theology, emphasizing moral repentance and forgiveness.

- Jain Approach: Focuses on karma and the consequences of actions.

- Leftist Approach: Critiques the concept of sin as a tool for social control, arguing for a focus on systemic change rather than individual moral failing.

- Malay Muslim Approach: Interprets sin and redemption within Islamic teachings.

Depiction of Ayodhya:

- Valmiki: Ayodhya is portrayed as an ideal kingdom, with Rama's rule (Rama Rajya) being the epitome of dharma and prosperity.

- Bulcke's Missionary lens: Draw parallels between Ayodhya and the Kingdom of God, interpreting Rama Rajya as a metaphor for a divinely ordained moral order.

- Jain Approach: Focuses on the ethical governance of Ayodhya.

- Leftist Approach: Questions the portrayal of Ayodhya as an ideal society, pointing out social inequalities and the exclusion of marginalized communities within the narrative.

- Malay Muslim Approach: Adapts Ayodhya's depiction to local cultural narratives.

Lakshman's Loyalty:

- Valmiki: Lakshman's loyalty and dedication to Rama are central, depicting the ideal relationship between brothers.

- Bulcke's Missionary lens: Lakshman's loyalty is reflective of Christian notions of discipleship and unwavering faith.

- Jain Approach: Views Lakshman's loyalty through the lens of familial duty.

- Leftist Approach: Critiques Lakshman's loyalty as indicative of the feudal loyalty system, emphasizing the need for solidarity based on equality rather than hierarchical obedience.

- Malay Muslim Approach: May reinterpret Lakshman's loyalty in the context of local traditions.

Vanavasa (Exile) Theme:

- Valmiki: Rama's exile is a period of trial and adherence to dharma, demonstrating his commitment to righteousness even in hardship.

- Bulcke's Missionary lens: Interpret the exile as a journey of personal growth and spiritual purification, akin to Christian pilgrimages or trials of faith.

- Jain Approach: Focuses on the ethical trials during exile.

- Leftist Approach: Interprets the exile as a reflection of social injustice and the struggles of the dispossessed, advocating for resistance against unjust exile and displacement.

- Malay Muslim Approach: Adapts the exile narrative to local myths and moral lessons

Final Departure of Rama:

- Valmiki: Rama's ascension to heaven (Vaikuntha) is a divine return, marking the end of his earthly duties.

- Bulcke's Missionary lens: Draws analogies with the Christian concept of ascension, interpreting it as a fulfilment of divine mission and return to the divine realm.

- Jain Approach: Focuses on the karmic completion of Rama's journey.

- Leftist Approach: Questions the glorification of divine ascension, focusing instead on the material and historical implications of Rama's rule and its impact on the common people.

- Malay Muslim Approach: Reinterprets the final departure within Islamic eschatology.

Caste and Class Dynamics:

- Valmiki: Depicts a society of Treta Yuga with rigid caste hierarchies.

- Bulcke's Missionary lens: May not explicitly address caste.

- Jain Approach: Emphasizes ethical behaviour over caste distinctions.

- Leftist Approach: Critiques the Ramayana for perpetuating caste discrimination, advocating for a reading that highlights the struggles and voices of lower castes and oppressed classes.

- Malay Muslim Approach: Reinterprets caste dynamics through an Islamic lens.

Gender Roles and Patriarchy:

- Valmiki: Portrays traditional gender roles.

- Bulcke's Missionary lens: Emphasizes ethical dilemmas faced by women.

- Jain Approach: Highlights the spiritual equality of genders.

- Leftist Approach: Strongly criticizes the patriarchal elements in the Ramayana, particularly the treatment of Sita, Shurpanakha, and other female characters, advocating for feminist reinterpretations.

- Malay Muslim Approach: Adapts gender roles to align with Islamic teachings.

Ethnic and Regional Diversity:

- Valmiki: The diversity is related to the citizens of three kingdom, Ayodhya, Khishkinda and Lanka

- Bulcke's Missionary lens: Comparative and ethical focus.

- Jain Approach: Incorporates regional variations within Jain communities.

- Leftist Approach: Highlights the cultural and regional diversity within the Ramayana, challenging the dominance of the Aryan narrative and emphasizing the stories of marginalized communities.

- Malay Muslim Approach: Integrates local ethnic and cultural elements.

Symbolism of Characters:

- Valmiki: Characters symbolize various aspects of dharma and adharma (The Ramayana Secrets explores this in depth)

- Bulcke's Missionary lens: Characters symbolize moral and ethical principles.

- Jain Approach: Characters reflect Jain virtues and vices.

- Leftist Approach: Reinterprets characters to highlight social and political struggles.

- Malay Muslim Approach: Characters are adapted to fit local mythological symbolism.

Narrative Structure and Style:

- Valmiki: Epic poetry with a linear narrative.

- Bulcke's Missionary lens: Comparative analysis with a focus on ethical themes.

- Jain Approach: Jain narrative techniques and philosophical discourses.

- Leftist Approach: Emphasizes socio-political context and narrative critique.

- Malay Muslim Approach: Adapts narrative style to fit local storytelling traditions.

Additional Insights on Traditional Versions:

- **Valmiki's Ramayana**: Offers a comprehensive and nuanced portrayal of Rama's life, deeply rooted in principles of dharma and morality. This epic, rich in detail and character complexity, captures the human essence of its characters, providing extensive plot development. While primarily an epic narrative, it harmoniously integrates layered metaphoric and allegorical dimensions, like those explored in "Ramayana Secrets," providing a profound exploration of spiritual and ethical dilemmas and facts. (when written, not known since Valmiki was a contemporary of Lord Rama

- **Ramcharitmanas**: Focuses on bhakti (devotion) and presents Rama as the Supreme Being. The narrative is more devotional, idealized, and includes additional episodes and discourses on devotion and righteousness. (when written, around 1574 CE)

- **Kamba Ramayana**: Authored by Tamil poet Kambar, this rendition weaves the Ramayana into Tamil culture, emphasizing Rama's divinity and heroism. It includes local folklore, enriching the narrative with cultural resonance for Tamil audiences. Celebrated for its poetic finesse and emotional depth, the Kamba Ramayana delves into themes of devotion and duty, presenting them in a lyrically engaging manner. (when written, around 1220 CE)

- **Adhyatma Ramayana**: Emphasizes the spiritual and metaphysical dimensions of Rama's story, presenting it as a divine play. The narrative is more concise, philosophical, and includes discourses on Advaita Vedanta, with symbolic and allegorical elements. (Brahmanada Purana adaptation introduced 15th century CE)

These variations not only showcase the Ramayana's versatility but also its capacity to bridge ancient wisdom with contemporary questions of morality, spirituality, and human nature.

Appendix II

Unveiling the Ramayana as a Psychological Blueprint

The abstract interpretation of the Ramayana presented in this book is given below as a potential framework for a psychology theory, one that delves deeper into the human psyche than traditional Western approaches. It was felt necessary to explore this perspective, as many Western scholars have dismissed the Ramayana as a collection of disjointed stories, confusing and lacking a coherent framework. However, when viewed as an allegory of the inner human journey, the Ramayana reveals profound insights into the complexities of the mind, offering a holistic understanding of emotional, spiritual, and psychological development.

Introduction

The Ramayana, one of the greatest epics of ancient India, is revered not only as a historical and cultural narrative but also as a profound exploration of the human psyche. While Western psychology has developed various theories to understand human behaviour, cognition, and development, these theories also share a common goal: the pursuit of mental wellness. The Valmiki Ramayana, similarly, offers an insightful model of human behaviour, guiding individuals toward mental, emotional, and spiritual well-being. In this chapter, we will explore the parallels between Western psychology theories and the abstract psychological model presented in the Ramayana, culminating in how the epic's teachings, combined with the devotional practices of living Hinduism, provide a comprehensive approach to achieving a fulfilling and self-realized life.

Section 1: Essentials of Western Psychology Concepts

Western psychology has evolved through various schools of thought, each contributing unique perspectives on human behaviour, development, and mental wellness. Here are some of the most influential theories:

1. Psychoanalytic Theory (Sigmund Freud)

Freud's theory posits that human behaviour is driven by unconscious forces, primarily rooted in sexuality and aggression. The mind is divided into three parts: the id (instinctual desires), the ego (rational thought), and the superego (moral standards). Freud believed that mental wellness is achieved by resolving the conflicts between these forces through psychoanalysis.

2. Behaviourism (John B. Watson, B.F. Skinner)

Behaviourism emphasizes that behaviour is learned through interactions with the environment, with reinforcement and punishment playing key roles. This theory focuses on observable behaviour rather than internal mental states, suggesting that mental wellness can be attained by modifying behaviour through conditioning.

3. Humanistic Psychology (Carl Rogers, Abraham Maslow)

Humanistic psychology centres on the inherent goodness of individuals and their potential for growth. It emphasizes self-actualization—the process of realizing one's full potential—as the goal. This theory advocates for free will and the human capacity for self-determination and the pursuit of meaning, proposing that mental wellness is achieved through personal growth and fulfilment.

4. Cognitive Psychology (Jean Piaget, Aaron Beck)

Cognitive psychology explores how people perceive, think, and solve problems. It examines the mental processes that underlie behaviour, such as memory, perception, and problem-solving. Cognitive theories highlight the importance of thought patterns and beliefs in shaping emotions and behaviours, suggesting that mental wellness depends on healthy cognitive processes.

5. Evolutionary Psychology (David Buss, Leda Cosmides)

Evolutionary psychology proposes that many human behaviours are adaptive traits shaped by natural selection. It suggests that our psychological mechanisms evolved to solve problems related to survival and reproduction, providing an evolutionary basis for certain behaviours. Mental wellness, in this context, is linked to how well individuals adapt to their environment.

6. Social Psychology (Kurt Lewin, Leon Festinger)

Social psychology studies how individuals are influenced by their social environment. It examines group dynamics, social interactions, and cultural norms, revealing how social context shapes behaviour and attitudes. Mental wellness is seen as being heavily influenced by social connections and cultural integration.

7. Developmental Psychology (Jean Piaget, Erik Erikson)

Developmental psychology focuses on the growth and changes that occur throughout a person's life, proposing that individuals go through distinct stages of cognitive, emotional, and social development. Mental wellness is achieved by successfully navigating these developmental stages.

8. Biopsychology/Neuroscience

This approach investigates the biological underpinnings of behaviour, exploring how brain structures, neurotransmitters, and genetics influence mental processes and actions. Mental wellness is seen as a balance of neurological health and proper brain function.

9. Jungian Psychology (Carl Jung)

Jungian psychology emphasizes the role of the unconscious, including the collective unconscious and archetypes, in shaping human behaviour. Jung believed that mental wellness is achieved through the process of individuation, where one integrates different aspects of the self, both conscious and unconscious, to achieve wholeness and by which an individual becomes distinct and separate from others

Each of these theories provides valuable insights into different aspects of the human experience, from unconscious drives to social influences, and from cognitive development to biological processes. At their core, these theories share a common goal: the pursuit of mental wellness

Section 2: The Valmiki Ramayana Model of Human Behaviour

The Valmiki Ramayana, while primarily a spiritual and moral epic, can also be interpreted as a profound exploration of human behaviour and psychology, with a similar goal of achieving mental and spiritual well-being. The characters in the Ramayana symbolize various aspects of the human psyche, and their interactions reflect the internal struggles and developmental processes that individuals experience in their quest for wholeness.

1. Rama as the Higher Self

Rama represents the higher self or the ideal human being—righteous, wise, and aligned with dharma (cosmic law and order). He embodies the qualities of self-control, moral integrity, and spiritual wisdom. In psychological terms, Rama symbolizes the ego functioning at its best, guided by ethical principles and a clear sense of purpose, much like the goal of self-actualization in humanistic psychology.

2. Sita as Faith and Purity (Shakthi)

Sita symbolizes faith, purity, and the inner voice that guides individuals toward their higher purpose. Her abduction by Ravana represents the loss of this guiding faith due to the influence of negative impulses and external temptations, echoing the internal conflicts described in psychoanalytic theory.

3. Ravana as the Lower Self

Ravana embodies the lower self—ego-driven, hedonistic, and corrupt. He represents the base instincts and desires that lead to moral decay and spiritual downfall, paralleling the destructive forces of the id in Freud's theory. Ravana's actions throughout the epic illustrate the psychological and spiritual dangers of unchecked ambition and desire.

4. Hanuman as Devotion and Focus

Hanuman symbolizes devotion, courage, and unwavering focus on the higher self. His loyalty to Rama represents the power of bhakti (devotion) in overcoming obstacles and staying true to one's spiritual path. Hanuman's feats, such as leaping across the ocean to find Sita, highlight the strength that comes from aligning oneself with divine will, much like the process of individuation in Jungian psychology.

5. The Battle as an Inner Struggle

The epic battle between Rama and Ravana can be seen as an allegory for the inner conflict between the higher and lower selves. This struggle is timeless, reflecting the ongoing challenge of maintaining righteousness and overcoming the temptations and desires that lead one astray. This mirrors the concept of balancing the conscious and unconscious aspects of the self in Jungian theory.

6. The Churning of the Internal Milky Ocean

The metaphor of the "churning of the internal milky ocean" represents the process of self-discovery and personal growth. Just as the gods and demons churned the ocean to bring forth divine treasures, individuals must churn their inner selves—examining their thoughts, emotions, and actions—to uncover the wisdom and virtues within. This process is akin to the psychological journey of individuation, where one integrates different aspects of the self to achieve mental wellness and spiritual enlightenment.

In this model, the Ramayana offers timeless lessons on human behaviour, emphasizing the importance of self-control, devotion, and the pursuit of dharma. It provides a framework for understanding the complexities of the human psyche and the challenges of personal growth, much like the theories in Western psychology.

Section 3: The Power of Devotional Practices in Living Hinduism

While the Ramayana offers profound psychological insights, it is through the devotional practices of living Hinduism that these lessons are fully integrated into daily life. Kirtan, meditation, and pilgrimage are powerful tools that help individuals internalize the teachings of the Ramayana and achieve a fulfilling, self-realized life, ultimately leading to mental wellness and spiritual growth.

1. Kirtan (Devotional Singing)

Kirtan involves the communal singing of hymns and praises to the divine. This practice not only fosters a sense of community but also helps individuals connect emotionally and spiritually with the higher self. Through the repetition of divine names and stories, kirtan reinforces the values and principles embodied in the Ramayana, making them a living part of the participant's consciousness, much like cognitive-behavioural therapy encourages the repetition of positive thought patterns.

2. Meditation

Meditation is a central practice in Hinduism that allows individuals to quiet the mind and connect with their inner self. By focusing on mantras or the image of the divine, practitioners can cultivate a deeper awareness of their thoughts and emotions, leading to greater self-control and spiritual insight. Meditation helps integrate the higher qualities symbolized by Rama into everyday life, enabling individuals to navigate challenges with clarity and wisdom, akin to the mindfulness practices that promote mental wellness in Western psychology.

3. Pilgrimage

Pilgrimage to sacred sites associated with the Ramayana, such as Ayodhya or Rameswaram, offers a powerful means of spiritual renewal. These journeys allow individuals to step away from the distractions of daily life and immerse themselves in the sacred narratives of the epic. Pilgrimage fosters a deep connection with the divine and reinforces the lessons of the Ramayana, offering a transformative experience that can lead to lasting personal growth, much like the therapeutic journey toward self-actualization or individuation.

Conclusion: The Superiority of a Devotional Life

The Ramayana, when viewed through the lens of psychology, offers valuable lessons on human behaviour and the inner journey toward mental wellness. However, it is through the devotional practices of kirtan, meditation, and pilgrimage that these teachings are fully realized. Living Hinduism provides a holistic approach to life that not only addresses the mind and body but also nourishes the soul. By engaging in these practices, individuals can align themselves with their higher self, overcome the lower impulses symbolized by Ravana, and achieve a life that is both fulfilling and spiritually realized. In this way, the Ramayana's teachings are not just theoretical concepts but practical tools for living a life of dharma and inner peace. This approach, which combines the wisdom of the Ramayana with powerful devotional practices, offers a superior and necessary path to achieving a life that is both mentally well and spiritually fulfilled.

Appendix III

Caste and Gender in the Ramayana: Beyond the Surface

In modern discourse, the Ramayana has often been critiqued for its portrayal of caste and gender, with some interpreting its narratives as reinforcing social hierarchies and gender inequalities. Yet, to truly understand the epic, it is essential to look beyond these surface-level interpretations and delve into the symbolic meanings that Valmiki intended to convey.

Caste in the Ramayana: A Complex Portrayal

The role of caste in the Ramayana is a topic of considerable debate. One of the most controversial episodes is the Shambuka narrative, found in the Uttara Kanda. Shambuka, a Shudra (a member of the lower caste), is depicted performing penance, an act traditionally reserved for the higher castes. When a Brahmin child dies prematurely, the cause is attributed to Shambuka's actions, leading Rama to kill him to restore cosmic order. This story has been criticized for its apparent endorsement of caste boundaries. However, this interpretation might overlook the allegorical nature of the Ramayana, where characters and events often symbolize broader spiritual and moral concepts rather than rigid social structures.

Adding complexity to the caste narrative is the fact that Ravana, the epic's primary antagonist, is a Brahmin by birth, while Rama, the hero, is a Kshatriya. These dynamic challenges the notion that the Ramayana is merely a reflection of caste-based discrimination. Ravana's downfall is not a result of his caste but rather his embodiment of ego, desire, and moral corruption—universal flaws that transcend social hierarchies. This indicates that the Ramayana's teachings are less about enforcing caste divisions and more about highlighting the ethical qualities that define individuals.

The epic also portrays characters like Guha, the Nishada king, and the Vanaras, who, despite their lower social status, are instrumental in aiding Rama. These examples suggest that the Ramayana values virtue and loyalty over caste, challenging the view that the epic rigidly enforces social hierarchies.

Gender in the Ramayana: A Deeper Look

Gender roles in the Ramayana have also been a point of contention, particularly in the portrayal of female characters like Sita. Sita, the epitome of loyalty and virtue, undergoes severe trials, including the Agni Pariksha (trial by fire) and later exile due to public suspicion about her purity. While these episodes have been criticized for reflecting societal expectations that place undue burdens on women, they also serve to underscore the epic's emphasis on dharma—righteousness and duty—even in the face of personal suffering.

Other female characters, such as Kaikeyi and Surpanakha, further illustrate the complexity of gender roles in the Ramayana. Kaikeyi, who manipulates events to ensure her son

Bharata's ascension to the throne, is often viewed negatively. Yet, her actions also highlight the limited power and influence women had in royal politics, often resorting to indirect means to assert their will.

Surpanakha, Ravana's sister, represents unchecked desire and inappropriate relations. Her pursuit of Rama and Lakshman leads to her humiliation and disfigurement, serving as a moral lesson on the consequences of desire that violates social and ethical boundaries.

Similarly, characters like Tataka, who symbolizes destructive tendencies, and Ahalya, who is redeemed by Rama after being turned to stone for adultery, illustrate that the Ramayana's lessons are not confined to gender but are broader reflections on human behaviour and moral integrity.

Ravana, Tataka, and Surpanakha: Symbolism Over Literalism

Modern critiques that frame the Ramayana as perpetuating casteism or misogyny often miss the symbolic depth of these characters. Ravana, though a Brahmin, embodies traits like ego and moral corruption, which the epic condemns, not because of his caste, but because of his unethical behaviour. Similarly, Tataka and Surpanakha represent more than just individuals—they symbolize broader, destructive tendencies within human nature.

Tataka's portrayal as a cannibalistic demon represents unchecked, destructive forces, while Surpanakha's inappropriate advances toward Rama and Lakshman symbolize the dangers of violating social and moral boundaries. These characters are not merely vilified for their actions but are used to convey deeper moral lessons about the consequences of succumbing to lower impulses.

Aryan-Dravidian Divide: A Misguided Construct

The theory of an Aryan-Dravidian divide was introduced in the 19th century by Western historians and linguists who sought to explain the linguistic and cultural diversity of India. According to this theory, the "Aryans," depicted as light-skinned invaders from Central Asia, supposedly conquered the darker-skinned "Dravidians," who were the original inhabitants of the Indian subcontinent. This theory suggested that the Vedic civilization, and by extension the epics like the Ramayana, were products of this supposed Aryan dominance.

This narrative conveniently aligned with the colonial agenda of divide and rule, fostering divisions between different communities in India. By framing the cultural and religious texts of India as the products of an invading Aryan elite, this theory undermined the deep-rooted unity and shared heritage of the subcontinent. It also imposed a racial lens on Indian history, which was alien to the indigenous understanding of identity, which is based more on varna (class or duty) and jati (occupational community) rather than race.

Western Misinterpretations:

The introduction of the Aryan-Dravidian divide also reflected a deeper insecurity within the Western psyche. Faced with the richness and antiquity of Indian civilization, which boasted advanced knowledge in mathematics, astronomy, medicine, and philosophy, the colonial powers found it difficult to accept the possibility that the Indian subcontinent had nurtured such profound intellectual and spiritual achievements independently. To reconcile this, they constructed a narrative where the "superior" Aryan race brought civilization to India, downplaying the indigenous contributions to the world's knowledge systems.

This divide was further emphasized by the misinterpretation of ancient texts. Western scholars, unfamiliar with the symbolic and allegorical nature of epics like the Ramayana, often reduced these narratives to simplistic tales of racial conflict. They interpreted the conflicts between characters as reflections of a racial struggle, rather than the deeper moral and spiritual battles that these stories represent.

Western Criticism of the Ramayana: Ignorance or Agenda?

Scholars like Audrey Truschke, Wendy Doniger, and Sheldon Pollock have critiqued the Ramayana through post-colonial, feminist, or Marxist frameworks, often interpreting the epic as reinforcing patriarchal values and caste hierarchies. However, these perspectives tend to overlook the deeper, spiritual layers embedded in the narrative. The Ramayana is not merely a historical or literal recounting of events but a profound, multilayered tale that explores the eternal struggle between dharma (righteousness) and adharma (unrighteousness), as well as the journey of self-realization. Through its characters and allegories, the Ramayana reveals deeper truths about the human condition, transcending superficial critiques of social structures and embodying a timeless narrative about spiritual evolution and ethical living.

While academic critique is essential for progress, the danger lies in distorting sacred texts without fully understanding their cultural and spiritual contexts. The Ramayana—a story that has endured for centuries—offers lessons far more profound than these critiques suggest. It conveys universal truths about virtue, spirituality, and the cosmic order. Reducing the epic to Western frameworks of power and social dynamics overlooks its true essence.

These critiques may stem from a colonial legacy of undermining Hindu traditions, often driven by an agenda to misinterpret spiritual texts. Ultimately, the Ramayana is a timeless guide, revered for its teachings on righteousness and spirituality, which cannot be captured adequately through reductionist interpretations.

Dismantling the Divide: The Unity of Indian Civilization

When we look beyond this imposed narrative, the Ramayana and other epics reveal a far more complex and unified vision of Indian civilization. The characters and events in these texts are not representations of racial or ethnic groups but are symbolic of universal human qualities and struggles.

In the Ramayana, the conflicts are not between different races but between different aspects of human nature. Rama and Ravana are not representatives of opposing races; they symbolize the eternal struggle between dharma (righteousness) and adharma (unrighteousness). The so-called Aryan-Dravidian divide dissolves when we understand that these epics are concerned with the inner battles each individual faces, rather than external conflicts between different peoples.

Moreover, the Ramayana's depiction of various regions and peoples—including the Vanaras of Kishkindha, the Rakshasas of Lanka, and the citizens of Ayodhya—does not suggest a racial hierarchy but rather a moral and spiritual landscape where individuals and communities are judged by their adherence to dharma. The unity of the Indian subcontinent, as reflected in the Ramayana, is based on shared values and spiritual goals, not on racial or ethnic divisions.

A Call to Recognize the Shared Heritage

The Aryan-Dravidian divide has been used as a tool to fracture the understanding of India's past, but the hidden meanings in the Ramayana and other epics dismantle this divisive narrative. These texts celebrate the unity of human experience and the shared spiritual journey that transcends superficial differences. They emphasize the common values that bind diverse communities together—values of truth, justice, and the pursuit of a higher purpose.

As we move forward, it is essential to reject these outdated and divisive constructs and to embrace the true spirit of the Ramayana—a spirit that sees beyond external differences and recognizes the shared heritage of all people in Bharat Varsha. By understanding the Ramayana in its true context, we can appreciate the profound unity that underlies the diversity of Indian civilization, a unity that has withstood the test of time and continues to inspire millions today.

The Ramayana, with its rich allegories and profound teachings, offers a powerful counter-narrative to the Aryan-Dravidian divide. It reminds us that our greatest battles are not with each other, but within ourselves. The true victory lies in overcoming the divisions within our own hearts, leading to a society where unity, compassion, and dharma prevail.

Conclusion: A Timeless Narrative with Universal Lessons

The Ramayana, while rooted in the social context of its time, transcends the limitations of caste and gender interpretations. By examining the deeper symbolic meanings of its characters and narratives, it becomes clear that the epic is not merely a reflection of ancient societal norms but a timeless exploration of the human condition.

The portrayal of Ravana as a Brahmin, Rama as a Kshatriya, and the symbolic roles of characters like Tataka and Surpanakha challenge the simplistic view that the Ramayana reinforces casteism and misogyny. Instead, the epic offers universal lessons on the ethical and spiritual qualities that define human behaviour.

In a world where the Ramayana continues to be a source of inspiration and moral guidance, it is crucial to approach it with an understanding of its allegorical nature. The epic's true focus is on the internal struggles and moral dilemmas faced by individuals, regardless of caste or gender, making it a narrative that resonates with timeless relevance. The Ramayana's enduring appeal lies in its ability to guide us through life's complexities, offering wisdom that transcends the boundaries of time, caste, and gender.

Appendix IV

The Historic Ramayana

Why is there a need to establish the Historic authenticity of Ramayana?

After having explored the Ramayana at an abstract level in this book, revealing that its events represent the evolution of human consciousness, it is essential to also address the physical history of the epic. In South Asia, numerous locations correspond with the descriptions in the Ramayana with uncanny accuracy, suggesting a historical basis for the events. This alignment raises the question: if the Ramayana is merely a spiritual allegory, how can these tangible locations exist, tied so closely to the narrative?

Establishing the physical history of the Ramayana takes on even greater significance given the colonial and missionary forces that sought to undermine India's cultural unity. During their rule, these powers aimed to dismiss the *itihasas* as mere myths, branding them as superstitious mumbo-jumbo. This tactic served to portray India as a land in need of "civilization" under Western guidance, facilitating the extraction of its wealth and resources. The portrayal of India's sacred texts as fragmented and unreliable narratives played into the colonial agenda of dividing the Indian subcontinent, making it easier to govern.

This sly ploy by colonial and Abrahamic establishments not only sought to weaken the cultural identity of the region but also dismissed the profound historical, spiritual, and cultural depth found in the Ramayana. By establishing the physical history of the Ramayana, we challenge these distortions, reaffirming the epic's role in shaping a unified India and countering centuries of misrepresentation. Understanding both the metaphysical and historical aspects of the Ramayana helps reclaim its true significance for modern Hindus and offers a more complete understanding of this timeless narrative.

How do the hidden archeoastronomy clues in the Ramayana, along with the current state of archaeology in the Indian subcontinent, evoke a deeper understanding of its ancient roots and spiritual significance, even with minimal excavation?

The Ramayana weaves together not only a spiritual and moral narrative but also integrates astronomical clues to anchor key events in time. These astronomical markers, particularly in relation to the birth of Rama, the changing seasons, and geographic descriptions, provide insights into the era in which these events might have occurred. For instance, the description of Rama's birth in Valmiki Ramayana refers to specific planetary positions and celestial phenomena, such as the star Punarvasu in the zodiac sign Cancer, which has been calculated by some modern researchers to place Rama's birth over 12,000 years BC. The alignment of planets like Jupiter and the Moon further supports these ancient timeframes, adding a layer of historical specificity to the narrative.

Similarly, the epic contains vivid descriptions of seasonal changes as the characters move through various regions. For example, the monsoon season is extensively detailed during the Vanavas (exile) period, especially in Panchavati and Kishkindha, providing natural timelines and context to the events unfolding. In fact, Valmiki's poetic descriptions of seasons align with the monsoon rhythms and the agricultural cycles of the time, illustrating the deep connection between natural phenomena and human experience.

In addition to astronomical markers, the Ramayana references numerous rivers, lands, and regions that correspond to present-day geography. Rivers like the Ganga, Sarayu, Yamuna, Godavari, Mandakini, Tamasa, and Pampa are frequently mentioned, along with landmarks like the Dandakaranya forest and Chitrakoot. These descriptions provide an invaluable connection between ancient narratives and actual locations, validating the continuity of India's landscape through time.

Despite the wealth of cultural and geographical details, the quest for archaeological evidence has yielded only a fraction of India's ancient history, as the depth of excavations is minuscule in comparison to the vast historical timeline that the Ramayana represents. Ancient layers of civilization may remain unexplored. But for most Indians, this physical validation is not necessary.

The Aryan Invasion Theory and the Caucasian origin of the Aryans have been discredited by modern genetic studies, and the divide between Aryans and Dravidians has also been largely debunked. Genetic evidence points toward a shared heritage, confirming that these so-called divisions were manufactured narratives introduced during the colonial era.

However, the notion of a united India challenges those with vested interests in keeping the country divided. Modern-day "breaking India" forces, as articulated by thinkers like Rajiv Malhotra, continue to push for fragmentation along cultural and regional lines, often using outdated theories.

The deeper study of the Ramayana—its astronomical clues, cultural continuity, and profound narrative—stands as a powerful reminder of India's unity, both in its ancient past and its ongoing future.

Could the existence of Nal Setu, Vanaras, and the legacy of Chiranjeevi Hanuman reflect the deeper connection between physical evidence and the spiritual layers of the Ramayana, highlighting devotion and inner transformation?

The Nal Sethu, also known as Adam's Bridge as named by British, has long been a subject of fascination, with many identifying it as the bridge built by Lord Rama's Vanara army in the Ramayana. This bridge is described in the Valmiki Ramayana as a manmade structure built by the Vanara chief Nala, using rocks, tree trunks, and boulders to create a passage from India to Sri Lanka. Interestingly, satellite imagery from NASA has revealed the presence of a submerged land bridge, which stretches from the coast of Tamil Nadu, India, to the northern tip of Sri Lanka. The geological structure is believed to be a naturally occurring ridge, yet over this natural formation, there are remnants of what appears to be manmade walkways, suggesting that human intervention may have played a role in its construction.

While the archaeological layers of the bridge and other related sites have not been fully excavated, these findings offer a striking similarity to the descriptions in the Ramayana, further solidifying the belief that the epic has a strong foundation in historical events. For Hindus, the Ramayana has always been regarded as a real and integral part of their cultural and spiritual history. Thus, the necessity of proving its authenticity through scientific excavation is not a priority for most. The epic serves not only as a sacred text but also as a reflection of the evolution of the human psyche, as explored in this book.

This belief is further validated by the presence of numerous pilgrimage sites that have drawn seekers and devotees for millennia, underscoring the timeless connection between the story and the land. The unity of India, despite its immense diversity, is deeply rooted in the shared cultural heritage that texts like the Ramayana represent. It is a narrative that has inspired generations—from diplomats to scientists— showing how deeply ingrained figures like Hanuman are in the collective consciousness. Hanuman, representing devotion and unwavering service to the divine, resonates with people across all walks of life as a symbol of loyalty and strength in overcoming obstacles, whether personal or societal.

In this context, the call of "Jai Bajrangbali" continues to echo across the centuries, a testament to the spiritual and cultural unity fostered by the Ramayana. It is this intangible connection to the sacred that sustains India's unity, making further validation through archaeological evidence unnecessary for those who understand the profound lessons embedded in the epic.

The story of Hanuman's devotion, the conquest of Ravana, and the creation of the bridge are symbolic of humanity's spiritual journey, transcending the need for physical proof. The abstract understanding that the Ramayana embodies the evolution of the human mind, moving beyond ego and materialism toward divine alignment, is what holds lasting importance.

Why shouldn't a sacred text include examples of monkeys, bears, ghouls, and flying machines while teaching the importance of divine unity?

The approach embraced in the sacred epics like the Ramayana —where humans coexist with monkeys, bears, ghouls, and flying machines, all bound by a pursuit of divine unity—

represents a more evolved and inclusive way for the world to operate. It promotes diversity, plurality, and acceptance, in stark contrast to a rigid, monoculture or monotheistic "my way or the highway" mindset, which has historically fuelled intolerance and bigotry. The ability to weave together various beings, cultures, and paths within a unifying narrative is a profound reflection of the richness of Hindu philosophy, which acknowledges the complexity of life and the multiplicity of paths toward enlightenment.

The so-called "mythology" of these sacred epics offers far deeper truths about human existence and the spiritual journey than many "direct words from the divine" proposed by exclusive dogmatic traditions. In fact, these epics are not myths, but "sacred realities," which are grounded in the essence of human experience and spiritual evolution. Therefore, rather than viewing them as outdated stories, we should consider them "Dharma Epics"—timeless guides for navigating life's complexities while cultivating tolerance, harmony, and self-realization.

"A Guide for Young Adults with its Timeless Wisdom"

The Ramayana offers timeless wisdom crucial for guiding modern youth towards a purposeful and ethical life. The epic underscores the importance of adhering to principles (dharma), demonstrating through its characters—especially Rama—how to embody integrity and serve as societal role models. It stresses the importance of maintaining strong, supportive relationships, as illustrated by Rama's interactions with his brothers and allies. These narratives highlight the significance of mutual support and loyalty, teaching resilience and adaptability through hardships like Rama's exile, which, rather than breaking him, fostered reflection, alliances and growth.

The Ramayana also emphasizes maintaining one's cultural roots while adapting to new environments, showing that personal decisions should benefit both the individual and society. This epic not only inspires self-reliance but also highlights the importance of being a supportive community member, making it an invaluable resource for young adults striving to balance personal success with social responsibility.

Valmiki's Ramayana represents an inner journey that unfolds within each of us during our life. Rama symbolizes the ever-present divine force, ready to guide us as we align with our higher self. The Vanaras represent the restless, untamed mind that, when disciplined, can help conquer the inner Ravanas—our lower instincts like pride and selfishness. This daily process of inner conflict and spiritual growth reveals that the Ramayana is not just an ancient epic or a specific war that happened in the past but ongoing daily, Hence a timeless guide for our personal and spiritual evolution. That explains its intuitive attraction and fascination across regions and time

"Why 'Ramayana Secrets' is Essential Reading for All"

"Ramayana Secrets" delves into the deep spiritual and ethical lessons of the Ramayana, making its timeless wisdom accessible to a broad audience, including believers, sceptics, and those on a journey of self-discovery.

This book reinterprets ancient narratives to illuminate universal truths about human nature, purpose, and spirituality, appealing to anyone seeking deeper understanding and personal growth.

Whether you are a devout follower, a curious sceptic, or simply exploring spiritual concepts, "Ramayana Secrets" offers a fresh perspective that bridges traditional storytelling with contemporary relevance. It provides practical insights for managing stress and enhancing mental well-being, while also fostering a greater appreciation for loyalty, duty, and the intrinsic values that govern a fulfilling life.

This makes it an invaluable resource for enhancing self-awareness, promoting ethical living, and guiding readers towards a more purposeful existence.

Valmiki's Ramayana the epic is not confined to a specific time but is a narrative that unfolds within us every day. Rama symbolizes the ever-present divine force within, ready to manifest when needed. Our minds, often wild and untamed like the Vanaras (monkeys), can be aligned with our higher self, enabling us to conquer the Ravanas within—our lower instincts, pride, and selfishness. This ongoing process in our daily lives affirms that the Ramayana is not just a story of the past but a living guide for personal and spiritual evolution.

About the Author

Ramesh Krishnakumar is a marine professional with an engineering and technical background, who has always been deeply fascinated by Indian philosophy, Vedanta, and ancient models of wisdom. He firmly believes that the itihasas, such as the Ramayana and Mahabharata, are not just collections of fantastic stories but profound spiritual guides with hidden layers of meaning.

For over a decade, he has been dedicated to maintaining a YouTube channel that translates Sanskrit hymns into English, making these ancient texts more accessible to a global audience. You can explore his channel here:

YouTube Channel

https://www.youtube.com/channel/UC6JYMqaNnU9p74-uzTXCqtQ

"Ramayana Secrets" is his first book, marking a new milestone in his passion for interpreting the wisdom of Indian culture. In addition to his philosophical pursuits, Ramesh is also passionate about the greening of the maritime industry and energy transition, actively engaging with these causes to promote a more sustainable future for the planet.